ILLUSTRATED WILDLIFE ENCYCLOPEDIA

ANIMALS
IN THE WILD

ILLUSTRATED WILDLIFE ENCYCLOPEDIA

ANIMALS
IN
THE WILD

MICHAEL CHINERY

LORENZ BOOKS

Contents

Life in the Wild

Well over a million different kinds or species of animals live on our planet. They range from the huge blue whale, weighing up to 152 tons, down to microscopic creatures so small that several could sit comfortably on the head of a pin. These animals display an equally wide range of behavior, but all have the same basic need for somewhere to live

Polar bears have thick fur so they can live in the Arctic where the temperature can drop as low as -58°F

that will provide them with food and some degree of protection or shelter. Because individual animals cannot live forever, they also need to be able to produce more of their own kind—otherwise the species would die out. The production of new generations is called reproduction and it usually involves the meeting and mating of a male and a female of the same kind. Some form of communication is necessary to bring the males and females together. Animals also communicate with each other to warn of danger or to tell each other about good food sources. Communication is especially well developed among insects, such as ants and many bees and wasps, which live in colonies and work together for the good of the whole community.

Most crocodiles live in freshwater habitats, such as rivers, lakes and marshes.

Somewhere to live

Animals have explored and colonized just about every place on earth, from the deepest and coldest oceans to the hottest deserts and the highest mountain tops. Only the permanent ice fields around the poles lack resident animals, although emperor penguins spend several months guarding their chicks on the bare Antarctic ice. Most species are associated with particular habitats, such as forests or deserts, and each species is generally well adapted to the conditions in which it lives. Camels, for example, have many adaptations that enable them to survive in hot, dry deserts: broad feet help them to walk on loose sand, long eyelashes keep the sand out of their eyes, and the animals can go without water for long periods. Many smaller desert animals avoid the heat by sleeping in burrows during the day and coming out to feed only during the cool of the night. Mammals living in cold environments usually have thick fur or a layer of insulating blubber under the skin.

Leaf insects are very hard to distinguish from the leaves on which they live.

Camouflage is another valuable adaptation, enabling animals to blend in with their surroundings and hide from their enemies. Some animals use camouflage to hide from their prey. The tiger's stripes and the leopard's spots break up their outlines and enable them to creep up on their victims without being seen.

Something to eat

Few animals can go for more than a few days without eating. Food provides energy and the building materials needed for growth. Most animals are plant eaters or herbivores. As well as the herds of grazing mammals, they include vast numbers of leaf-chewing and sap-sucking insects. Meat eaters or carnivores include spiders, lions and crocodiles, and then there are the omnivores—animals that eat both plant and animal matter. They include many household pests, such as rats, mice and cockroaches. Some insects have decidedly odd diets: dung, carpets, and solid wood are all eaten by various species.

Zebras eat mainly grass and, like all equids, they graze for many hours a day.

Rearing a family

Corals and some sea anemones can produce branches that break off and grow into a new individual, but this kind of reproduction is unusual in the animal kingdom. Most animals lay eggs or give birth to active babies. This usually happens after a male and female pair up and mate, although aphids and some other insects can give birth without mating. Most insects and fishes take no interest in their offspring at all, while at the other end of the scale mammals are fed milk from their mothers' bodies and many are given a lot of care. Young chimps and elephants, for instance, depend on their mothers for several years after they are born.

Talking to each other

The dawn chorus of spring and early summer is a well-known example of animal communication. The male birds sing to attract females and also to let other males know that a territory is occupied. Gibbons and several kinds of monkeys also make a lot of noise to warn their neighbors to keep away. Most kinds of animals emit some sort of signal to attract mates and many animals give out scents that excite the opposite sex. Parents and offspring also communicate with each other. Baby birds, for example, squawk when hungry, and the parents use various calls to warn their babies of danger.

What lies ahead?

A baby gorilla travels around on its mother's back until it is strong enough to walk by itself.

Animals that are well adapted to their habitats and good at finding food and evading their enemies are most likely to survive and produce more of their own kind. They will pass their good qualities to their offspring and the species as a whole will continue to flourish.

Animal Habitats

Animals live in a wide range of climates and habitats, from grasslands and vast tracts of forest, to rivers and deep oceans. This section explores the problems that animals face living in the wild and what they do to overcome these problems.

A Place to Live

Ever since life began, different species have competed with each other for food and living space. This competition has led to each kind of animal becoming more or less specialized for a particular way of life in certain surroundings, known as its habitat, which may be a woodland, a savanna grassland, a small pond or a vast ocean. Wherever it lives, the animal must be well suited to its habitat, otherwise it will not survive. Most animals keep to one kind of habitat, but some species can survive in different surroundings, so long as they can find food.

Wolves can live in a range of habitats, from forests to open areas. Most wolves live in cool, temperate parts of the world, but some live in the deserts of south-east Asia.

Weather conditions

The climate—the temperature and amount of rainfall in an area—is the major factor that determines whether animals can exist in a particular place. Life cannot exist where the temperature is permanently below 15°F or above 115°F, but there are species that survive at all temperatures between these limits. Bears and other mammals living in very cold places generally have thick fur to keep them warm, while whales living in cold seas have a thick layer of body fat, called blubber, beneath the skin. Some insects living in cold regions have a kind of antifreeze in their blood to prevent them from freezing solid.

Animals living in deserts have usually adapted their behavior to cope with the difficult conditions. Many hide away in burrows in the heat of the day and come out only at night when the air is cooler. Beetles that roam about by day often have long legs to keep their bodies off the burning hot sand.

The grey whale migrates some 6,000 miles between its summer feeding grounds and winter breeding grounds. Many other animals also migrate in order to find the perfect habitat.

All living things need water to survive, and this is a particular problem for animals that live in deserts. Most have internal adaptations to help them use water more efficiently. Some desert animals never need to drink because they get enough water from their food and use it very carefully.

Enough to eat

Climate is not the only thing that determines where an animal can live. Within a region of suitable climate, animals can survive only where they can find the right habitat, with the right kinds of plants or other animals to eat.

Snakes are found in many different sorts of habitat, from deserts to rainforests. Most snakes can only live in warm climates, however, as they need the sun's heat to maintain their body temperature.

Animals search for their food in several ways. Some animals or family groups of animals, such as elephants, roam freely through a habitat without having any fixed home. Most animals, however, keep within a certain area. A pride (group) of lions, for example, has a definite territory that it defends against other lions. A territory may be large or small, but it will be big enough to provide food for all the animals living in the group, and it will have somewhere safe for the animals to raise their young.

Summer and winter—the changing seasons

The cool and temperate regions of the world experience very different conditions in summer and winter. Many mammals cope with the change by growing thicker coats for winter, but some move to warmer places. Several kinds of whale make these long-distance journeys, which are called migrations. They move to tropical waters for the winter and have their babies, and then go back to the cooler waters in spring. But cold weather is not the only problem facing animals in winter. Food may be in short supply, especially in areas that get a lot of snow. Some animals, including the raccoon dog, overcome this problem by hibernating (sleeping through the winter). They gorge themselves in the summer, building up a layer of fat to help them survive the winter.

In temperate regions, many plants lose their leaves for the winter. Insects that feed on them often go into hibernation. This shield bug matches the bright green leaves in the summer and it remains well camouflaged in autumn by turning reddish-brown. During the winter, it hibernates in the fallen leaves.

Success story

Animals have been incredibly successful at adapting to different habitats and environments. Today, there is hardly any place on Earth—from the highest mountain peaks to the deepest oceans—that does not support some kind of animal life.

Beetle and Bug Environments

Our planet has a huge number of different habitats, and beetles and bugs are found in most of them. Like other insects, beetles and bugs usually live in hot, tropical regions or in mild, temperate areas. Some, though, can survive on snow-capped mountains or frozen icefields, in caves and even in hot springs. Other beetles and bugs are found in places with heavy rainfall, and a few tough species survive in deserts.

Beetles and bugs that live in very cold or very hot places often adapt their life cycle to cope with the extreme temperatures. Many survive the coldest or driest periods as eggs in the soil. In deserts, beetles and bugs tend to be active at night, when the air is cooler. The toughest species have adapted to survive for long periods without food or even water.

▲ A WARM HOME
Bedbugs are parasites that live and feed on warm-blooded animals. Some species suck human blood while others infest the homes of birds and furry mammals, or live among their feathers or fur. Kept warm by their host animal, some bedbugs can even survive in cold places such as the Arctic.

Did you know? Water boatmen can fly many miles to find a new home.

◀ LIFE IN THE WATER
Water boatmen are predatory bugs that have adapted to life in the water. They prey on all kinds of small water creatures, including tadpoles and tiny fish. They are also called backswimmers because they swim upside-down, using their long back legs rather like oars. The bugs come to the surface from time to time to renew their air supplies.

LIVING IN THE DARK ▶

This stilt-legged bug has adapted to pitch-black caves in the Caribbean. Its antennae and legs are long and thin, to help it to feel its way. The legs and antennae are also covered with hairs that can detect the slightest air currents, alerting the bug to the presence of other animals.

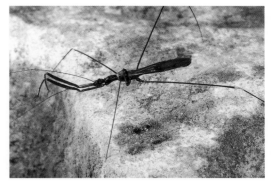

◀ DESERT SURVIVOR

The fog-basking beetle lives in the Namib Desert, in southern Africa. This beetle has an ingenious way of drinking. When fog and mist swirl over the dunes, it does a handstand and points its abdomen in the air. Moisture gathers on its body, then trickles down special grooves on its back into its waiting mouth.

NO CAMOUFLAGE REQUIRED ▶

This *Aphaenops* beetle lives in caves high in the Pyrenees mountains, between France and Spain. Its body is not well camouflaged but, in the dark of the caves, disguise is not important. Scientists believe some cave-dwelling species developed from beetles that first lived in the caves during the last Ice Age, about a million years ago.

dune beetle
(Onymacris bicolor)

◀ DUNE DWELLER

The dune beetle lives in the deserts of southern Africa. It is one of the few white beetles. White reflects the rays of the sun and helps to keep the insect cool. The pale color also blends in well with the sand where it lives, which helps it to hide from predators. The beetle's wing cases are hard and close-fitting, and so help to conserve precious body moisture in this dry region. Long legs raise the beetle's body above the burning hot desert sand.

13

Insects Living

SURFACE SPINNERS
Whirligig beetles are oval, flattened beetles that live on the surface of ponds and streams. Their eyes are divided into two, so that they can see above and below the water at the same time. The beetles are named after a spinning toy called a whirligig, because they swim in circles.

Some beetles and bugs live in and on fresh water—not only ponds and rivers but also icy lakes, muddy pools and stagnant marshes. Different types of water-dwellers live at different depths. Some live on or just below the water surface. Other species swim in the mid-depths, or lurk in the mud or sand at the bottom. Beetles and bugs that live underwater carry a supply of air down with them so that they can breathe.

In some other insects, only the larvae (young) live in the water, where there is plenty of food. The adults live on land.

SKATING ON WATER
Pond skaters live on the water surface. They move about like ice skaters on their long slender legs. The bugs' feet make dimples on the surface of the water, but do not break it. When the bugs sense a drowning insect nearby, they skate over in gangs to feed on it.

SPINY STRAW
A water scorpion has a long, hollow spine on its abdomen. The spine has no sting, but it is used to suck air from the surface. Sensors on the spine tell the bug when it is too deep to breathe.

In and On Water

THE AQUATIC SCORPION

Water scorpions are fierce predators. This bug has seized a stickleback fish in its pincer-like front legs. It then uses its mouthparts to pierce the fish's skin and suck out its juices. Compared to some aquatic insects, water scorpions are not strong swimmers. They usually move about by crawling slowly over submerged plants.

DIVING DEEP

Saucer bugs are expert divers. In order to breathe, the bug takes in air through spiracles (holes) in its body. Tiny bubbles of air are also trapped between the bug's body hairs, giving it its silvery colour. Saucer bugs use their front legs to grab their prey. They cannot fly, but move from pond to pond by crawling through the grass.

UNDERWATER ROWING

You can often see lesser water boatmen just below the water surface, but they can also dive further down. They use their back legs to row underwater, and breathe air trapped under their wings. The females lay their eggs on water plants or glue them to stones on the stream bed. The eggs hatch two months later.

Butterfly Habitats

orange-tip
butterfly
(*Anthocharis
cardamines*)

Almost every country in the world has its own particular range of butterflies and moths. They are surprisingly adaptable insects, and inhabit a huge variety of different environments, from the fringes of deserts to icy Arctic areas.

Butterflies and moths that live in cold climates tend to be darker than those living in warmer regions. This is because they need to be warm in order to fly, and dark colors soak up sunlight more easily. In mountainous areas, the local species usually fly close to the ground. Flying any higher than this would create a risk of being blown away by strong gusts of wind. Some female moths living in mountainous areas do not have wings at all, and move around by crawling along the ground.

◄ HEDGEROWS AND WAYSIDES

Orange-tip butterflies, named for the bright orange tips of the male's front wings, live in a wide range of grassy places, including hedgerows, woodland margins, damp meadows and roadsides. When at rest, with their front wings hidden behind the hind wings, their mottled green undersides blend in with the vegetation and make them very difficult to see.

apollo butterfly
(*Parnassius apollo*)

◄ HIGH LIFE

The apollo butterfly has adapted to life in the mountains of Europe and Asia. The apollo's body is covered with fur-like scales that protect it from the extreme cold. Most apollo eggs that are laid in autumn do not hatch until the following spring because of the low temperatures. Those caterpillars that do hatch hibernate at once.

◄ WETLAND WANDERER

The marsh fritillary butterfly flourishes among the flowers of open grassland in temperate regions (areas with warm summers and cold winters). It is happy in both damp and dry areas, but it needs plenty of warm sunshine in the spring to enable its caterpillars to develop properly.

BUTTERFLY HABITATS ▶

Some butterflies, such as the large white, occur in many habitats, including backyards. Others are more choosy about their homes. The grayling and Spanish festoon like coastal areas, while the speckled wood and white admiral prefer woodland glades. Arctic species include the moorland clouded yellow. The apollo and Cynthia's fritillary are alpine butterflies living high in mountains. Painted ladies inhabit many areas in summer, but spend the winter around the deserts of North Africa.

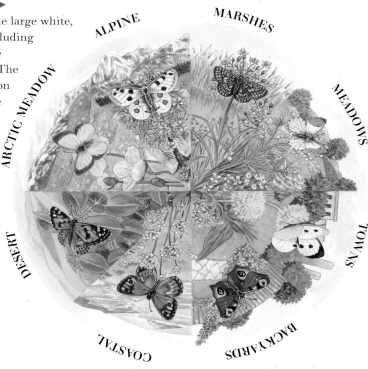

▼ GARDEN VISITORS

These peacock butterflies are feeding on a flower. Gardens provide food for all kinds of butterflies. Many flowers grown in gardens are related to wild roadside and field flowers.

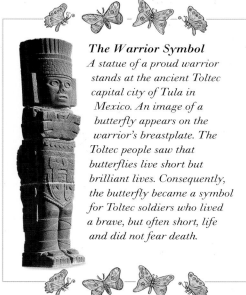

The Warrior Symbol

A statue of a proud warrior stands at the ancient Toltec capital city of Tula in Mexico. An image of a butterfly appears on the warrior's breastplate. The Toltec people saw that butterflies live short but brilliant lives. Consequently, the butterfly became a symbol for Toltec soldiers who lived a brave, but often short, life and did not fear death.

Migrant Butterflies

Most butterflies and moths live and die within a very small area, never moving far from their birthplace. However, a few species travel astonishing distances in search of food, or to escape cold or overpopulated areas.

migration path

Some butterfly species, such as the painted lady and monarch, are true migrants, following the same routes year after year. For individual butterflies, however, it's a one-way trip. Clouded yellow caterpillars, for example, feed in the Mediterranean region in spring. As adults, many fly northwards to feed and mate. There, they lay eggs and new generations can be seen throughout the summer. But the clouded yellow cannot survive the cold and, apart from the few that manage to get back to southern Europe, the butterflies die in the autumn.

▲ **THE ROYAL ROUTE**
Monarch butterflies migrate mainly between North and Central America. Occasionally, instead of flying south, strong winds can sweep the butterflies 3,500 miles north east, to Europe.

▲ **TREE REST**
Every autumn huge numbers of monarch butterflies leave Canada and the northern United States and fly 2,000 miles south to spend the winter in Mexico. They make the journey as quickly as possible, resting on trees on the way.

▲ **MONARCHS ON THE MOVE**
In spring, monarchs begin their journey north. They lay their eggs on the way and then die. Once their young become butterflies, the cycle begins again. The new butterflies either continue north or return south, depending on the season.

brown-veined white butterfly
(Belenois aurota)

◀ AN AFRICAN MIGRANT

This butterfly has large wings capable of carrying it over long distances. Millions of brown-veined white butterflies form swarms in many parts of southern Africa. A swarm can cause chaos to people attempting to drive through it. Although this butterfly flies throughout the year, the swarms are seen most often in December and January.

Did you know? A large swarm of migrating butterflies can bring farm machines to a standstill by resting on them.

FAST AS A HAWK ▶

Every spring thousands of oleander hawk moths set off from their native lands in tropical Africa and head north, over the Mediterranean sea. A few of them reach the far north of Europe in late summer. Hawk moths are among the furthest flying of all moths. They are able to travel rapidly over long distances.

oleander hawk moth
(Daphnis nerii)

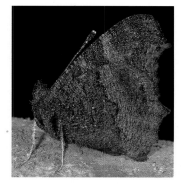

▼ CHASING THE SUN

The painted lady butterfly lives almost all over the world. In summer it is found across Europe, as far north as Iceland. However, it cannot survive the winter frosts in temperate areas. Adults emerging in late summer head south, and a few reach North Africa before the autumn chill starts.

painted lady butterfly
(Vanessa cardui)

▲ SURVIVING THE COLD

The adult peacock butterfly hibernates during the winter. The peacock is protected by chemicals called glycols that stop its body fluids from freezing. Many other moths and butterflies survive the winter by hibernating instead of migrating.

19

Spider Homes

There are few places on Earth that spiders do not live. They are found in forests, grasslands, marshes and deserts, on high mountain tops and hidden in caves. Even remote islands are inhabited by spiders, perhaps blown there on the wind or carried on floating logs. Many spiders live in our houses and some travel the world on cargo ships. Others make their home in city sewers, where there are plenty of flies for them to feed on. Spiders are not very common in watery places, however, as they cannot breathe underwater. There are no spiders in Antarctica, although some do live near the Arctic. To survive the winter in cool places, spiders may stay as eggs or hide under grass, rocks or bark. Some spiders even have a type of antifreeze to stop their bodies from freezing.

▲ **HEDGEROW WEBS**
One of the most common spiders on bushes and hedges in Europe and Asia is the hammock web spider. One hedge may contain thousands of webs with their haphazard threads.

Did you know? Some spiders live in the webs of other species of spider and steal their food.

◀ **SPIDER IN THE SINK**
The spiders that people sometimes find in the sink or the bathtub are usually male house spiders that have fallen in while searching for a mate. They cannot climb back up the smooth sides because they do not have gripping tufts of hair on their feet like hunting spiders.

▲ LURKING IN THE DARK
The cave orb-weaver almost always builds its web in very dark places, often suspended from the roof. It is found in caves, mines, hollow trees, railway tunnels, drains, wells and the corners of outbuildings in Europe, Asia and North America.

▲ LIVING IN A BURROW
The white lady spider lives in deserts. It hides away from the intense heat in a burrow beneath the sand. The main problem for desert spiders is lack of water. In times of drought the white lady spider may go into suspended animation, an extreme form of hibernation.

◄ HOSTILE HOME
This beach wolf spider is well camouflaged on the sand. It lives in a very hostile place. Waves pound on the beach and shift the sand. There is little fresh water and the sun quickly dries everything out. Food is scarce, although insects do gather on seaweed, rocks and plants growing along the edge of the shore.

RAINFOREST SPIDER ►
The greatest variety of spiders is found in tropical rainforests. Here, the climate is warm all year round and plenty of food is always available. This forest huntsman spider is well camouflaged against a tree trunk covered in lichen. To hide, it presses its body close against the tree. It lives in Malaysia where it is found in backyards as well as in the rainforest.

Snake Habitats

Every continent except Antarctica contains snakes, although they are most common in deserts and rainforests. Snakes cannot survive in very cold places because they use heat in the air around them to make their bodies work. Most snakes live in places where the temperature is high enough for them to stay active day and night. In cooler climates, snakes may spend the cold winter months asleep in hibernation.

▲ **OUT IN THE OPEN**
The European grass snake lives mainly on damp grassland. It sometimes climbs on to hedgerows to bask in the sunshine.

◄ **MOUNTAIN SURVIVAL**
The Pacific rattlesnake is sometimes found on the lower slopes of mountains in the western United States. In general, though, mountains are problem places for snakes because of their cold climates.

Pacific rattlesnake
(Crotalus viridis)

▲ **WINTER SLEEP**
Thousands of garter snakes emerge after their winter hibernation.

▼ **PLENTIFUL TROPICS**
Hot, tropical rainforests
contain the greatest
variety of
snakes, including
this Brazilian rainbow
boa. There is plenty to
eat in a rainforest,
from insects, birds
and bats to frogs.

▲ **FOREST LIFE**
This eyelash viper lives
in the Central American
rainforest. The climate here
is warm all year round, so
snakes can stay active all the
time. Snakes have adapted to
every niche provided by
the rainforest—there are
snakes in trees, on the
forest floor,
underground and
in rivers.

Brazilian rainbow boa
(Epicrates cenchria)

BARK TUNNEL ▶
Yellow-headed worm
snakes live under
tree bark. Other
worm snakes live
underground where
the soil is warm.

◀ **AT HOME IN THE DESERT**
This African puff adder lives in
the deserts of southern Africa.
Many snakes live in deserts
because they can survive with
little food and water.

Desert Snakes

Many snakes live in deserts, although the habitat is hot, dry and inhospitable. This is partly because snakes can survive for a long time without food. Mammals need energy from food to produce body heat, but reptiles take their heat from their surroundings. Snakes are also able to thrive in deserts because their waterproof skins stop them from losing too much water. During the hottest part of the day, and the bitterly cold nights, snakes shelter under rocks or in the ground—often in rodent burrows.

desert horned viper
(Cerastes cerastes)

▼ SCALE SOUND
If threatened, this viper makes a loud rasping sound by rubbing together jagged scales along the sides of its body. This warns predators to keep away.

► GO AWAY!
A rattlesnake warns enemies that it is dangerous by shaking the rattle in its tail. Desert snakes do not hiss because they would lose precious moisture through water vapor.

24

SAND SHUFFLER ▶

The desert horned viper is a master ambusher. It spreads its ribs to flatten its body and shuffles its way under the sand until it almost disappears and only its eyes and horns show. It strikes out at its prey from this position.

◀ DESERT MOVES

Many desert snakes, such as this Peringuey's viper, travel in a movement called sidewinding. As the snake moves, only a small part of its body touches the hot sand at any time. Sidewinding also helps to stop the snake sinking down into the loose sand.

◀ HIDDEN BOA

The colors of this sand boa make it hard for predators and prey to spot it among the rocks and sand. The snake's smooth, round body shape helps it to burrow down into the sand.

The Hopi Indians

This Native North American was a Hopi snake chief. The Hopi people used snakes in their rain dances to carry prayers to the rain gods to make rain fall on their desert lands.

Tropical

Near the Equator, in areas with plenty of sun and rain, tropical rainforests grow. They are dense jungles, teeming with life. The emerald tree boa lives in the rainforests of South America. Its green body is well camouflaged among the leaves. Like other tree snakes, it moves easily among the trees, at home high above the jungle floor.

UPSIDE-DOWN ATTACK
To catch a small mammal or bird, an emerald tree boa drapes its coils over a horizontal branch and hangs its head down. As soon as a victim comes within reach, it strikes. Once the snake has a firm hold with its teeth, it coils around its prey. The boa squeezes slowly until the animal stops breathing and dies. The snake swallows its victim head-first so that it slides down easily.

PATCHY OUTLINE
The creamy colored bands along the back of an emerald tree boa help to break up its outline and camouflage it in the dappled light.

SLIM SLITHERER
Tree boas are longer and slimmer than boas that live on the ground. Their streamlined shape and lightweight head help them to slither through the branches easily.

Tree Boas

emerald tree boa
(Corallus canina)

COLOR CHANGE

Young emerald tree boas are orange, pink or yellow when they are born. They gradually change to green in their first year by producing new color pigments in their skin. No one is sure why the young are a different color from the adults. They may live in different places and need their red coloring for effective camouflage.

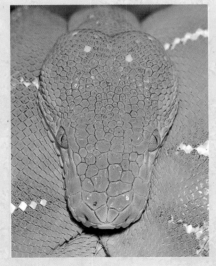

HOT LIPS

Heat-sensitive areas on the tree boa's lips help it to detect the warm-blooded animals on which it feeds.

LETHAL JAWS

The emerald tree boa can open its mouth very wide to swallow prey. Its sharp teeth slope backwards to grip the victim firmly and stop it escaping.

Crocodiles of Rivers and Lakes

Most crocodiles, alligators and other crocodilians prefer fresh water to salty water. They live in rivers, lakes and swamps, in warm climates. Crocodilians tend to live at the edge of the water because the shallows provide many plants to hide among and plenty of animals to eat.

Water is helpful in other ways, too. Like other reptiles, crocodilians draw their heat from their surroundings. Water helps to keep their body heat steady because the temperature of water does not vary as much as the temperature on dry land.

Crocodilians also save energy by moving about in rivers, because the water supports their heavy bodies. However, crocodilians can walk many miles on dry land. Young crocodilians may even gallop if they need to move quickly.

Aboriginal Creation Myth
Crocodiles are often shown in bark paintings and rock art made by the Aboriginals of Australia. Their creation myth, called the dream time, tells how ancestral animals created the land and people. According to a Gunwinggu story from Arnhem Land, the Liverpool River was made by a crocodile ancestor. The mighty crocodile made his way from the mountains to the sea, chewing the land as he went. This made deep furrows, which filled with water to become the river.

▲ **ALL-AMERICAN GATOR**
American alligators can be found on the southeastern coast of the United States, especially in Florida and Louisiana. The population of alligators cannot spread further north than Virginia or further west than Texas because the winters are too cold.

▲ **RIVER DWELLERS**
The gharial is a type of crocodilian that likes fast-flowing rivers, such as the Indus in Pakistan and the Ganges in India. It prefers rivers with high banks, clear water and deep pools where there are plenty of fish.

◄ CROWDED POOL

Caimans are a type of crocodilian from South America. During the dry season, they gather in the few remaining pools along drying-up river beds. Although the pools become very crowded, the caimans seem to get along well. In some areas, caimans are forced to live in river pools for four or five months of the year. After the floods of the wet season, they can spread out again.

SUN-LOVING NILE CROCODILES ►

These Nile crocodiles bask on the river banks to warm themselves after a night in the water. If they get too hot, they simply open their mouths and the evaporation from their huge mouths soon cools them down. If they still feel too hot, they simply slide into the water. Despite their name, these crocodiles live around many African lakes and rivers, not just the Nile.

◄ SHALLOW SWAMPS

This swamp is a billabong — a branch of a river that comes to a dead end. Billabongs provide crocodiles with water and land as well as food to eat. This one, in the Northern Territory of Australia, is home to Johnston's crocodiles. They lurk in shallow water, waiting to snap at fish, reptiles, birds and small mammals.

29

Saltwater Crocodiles

Most crocodilians live in fresh water, but some individuals venture into the salty water of estuaries (river mouths), and a few wander out into the sea. The species most likely to be seen at sea is the saltwater or estuarine crocodile. This is the world's biggest crocodile, and it grows up to 20 feet in length. It is found over a vast area, from India to northern Australia. Saltwater crocodiles are usually found in coastal rivers and swamps, but some have been seen swimming hundreds of miles from land. Some populations live entirely in the sea, and come ashore only to lay their eggs.

Living in salt water causes a problem for crocodiles. As they eat their food they swallow sea water, but they cannot cope with too much salt in their bodies. Crocodiles therefore have salt glands on their tongue that get rid of the extra salt.

▲ GETTING RID OF SALT

Saltwater crocodiles have up to 40 salt glands on the tongue. These special salivary glands allow the crocodile to get rid of excess salt. Freshwater crocodiles also have these glands, perhaps because their ancestors lived in the sea. Alligators and caimans do not have salt glands.

SCALY DRIFTER ▶

Although it can swim vast distances far out to sea, a saltwater crocodile is generally a lazy creature. Slow, side-to-side sweeps of a long, muscular tail propel it through the water, using as little energy as possible. Saltwater crocodiles do not like swimming vigorously, so they avoid strong waves wherever possible. They prefer to drift with the tide in relatively calm water.

NEW WORLD CROC ▶
The American crocodile is the most widespread crocodile in the Americas, ranging from southern Florida, to the Pacific coast of Peru. It is usually about ten feet long, although some grow up to 20 feet. The American crocodile often lives in brackish (slightly salty) water. It can be found in swamps, estuaries and lagoons as well as in rivers.

◀ TRAVELING CAIMANS
A group of baby spectacled caimans hides among the plants. This wide-ranging species lives mainly in muddy rivers but can tolerate salt marshes. Many caimans live on islands in the Caribbean, which their ancestors probably reached by swimming through the sea or by clinging to drifting logs.

◀ LOST ARMOR
A saltwater crocodile has less protective armor on the neck and back compared to other crocodilians. This makes it easier for the crocodile to bend its body when swimming. Thick, heavy scales would weigh it down too much at sea.

▲ ADVENTURE AT SEA
Nile crocodiles typically live in rivers, but they also inhabit salty estuaries. A strong current may sometimes sweep a crocodile out to sea. Some crocodiles survive these unplanned journeys and reach inhabitable islands.

31

Open Habitats for Birds of Prey

Many birds of prey make their home on grassland, moorland and other stretches of open land. Each species has adapted to a particular kind of habitat and to hunting the prey that is found there. This prevents too much competition for the food resources available. Imperial and golden eagles hunt in mountainous country. The gyrfalcon and snowy owl are the most successful predators on the bleak expanses of the Arctic tundra. Farmland provides a hunting ground for kestrels and harriers, while the vast savanna lands of eastern and southern Africa are the home of many vultures. Here, there are rich pickings on the carcasses of zebras and antelopes killed by large predators. Many vultures also hunt small prey themselves.

▲ GROUND NESTER
A young Montagu's harrier spreads its wings in the nest. Like other harriers, it nests in vegetation on the ground. This harrier lives on open moors and farmland throughout Europe, northern Africa and Asia.

Did you know? The lammergeier eats bones – it smashes them by dropping them from a great height.

◄ TUNDRA HUNTER
A gyrfalcon devours its prey. This bird lives in the cold, wide-open spaces of the Arctic tundra, in Alaska, northern Canada and northern Europe. The picture shows a young bird with dark, juvenile plumage. The adult is much paler – gray above and white underneath. Some birds are almost pure white and blend in perfectly with their snowy habitat.

▲ VULTURES AT THE CAPE

The Cape vultures of southern Africa inhabit the clifftops and hilly regions around the Cape of Good Hope. They have broad wings that enable them to soar effortlessly on the warm air currents rising from the hot land below. Often, several birds soar high in the air together, watching out for a meal to share.

▼ KILLING FIELDS

A common buzzard feeds on a dead rabbit that it has found. Buzzards live in open and lightly wooded country throughout the world. They can be found in both lowland and upland areas where their food — mainly small mammals — is plentiful.

◄ PLAINS WALKER

The secretary bird of Africa's savanna grassland is the only bird of prey that walks in search of prey. Its long legs enable it to search in all but the tallest grass, and the bird usually kills its prey by stamping on it.

▼ SUNNING ON THE SAVANNA

A young bateleur eagle suns itself on a tree in the savanna of Africa. When fully grown, it will fly over the grasslands all day, keeping a watchful eye for prey such as small mammals and reptiles.

bateleur eagle
(*Terathopius ecaudatus*)

Birds of Prey in Woods and Near Water

honey buzzard *(Pernis apivorus)*

The world's forests make good hunting grounds for many different kinds of birds of prey. The goshawk and sparrowhawk, and the common and honey buzzards, all make their homes in woodlands. Many owls prefer to live in woods, too. The most formidable forest predators, however, are the enormous South American harpy eagle and the Philippine eagle. They live in rainforests and prey on monkeys high in the treetops.

Lakes, rivers and estuaries are the territory of the sea and fishing eagles and the osprey. They have rough scales on their feet to help them grip slippery fish. In Asia and Africa, the fishing owls make their homes in woodlands close to the coast or by inland waterways.

▲ **FOREST FEEDER**
The honey buzzard is quite a small bird, found in the forests of Europe. Its bill is small and delicate compared to other raptors, well suited to its diet of the larvae of bees and wasps.

◄ **IN THE MARSHES**
Three marsh harrier chicks peep out of their reed nest in a swampy region of Poland. This species is the largest harrier, measuring up to 21 inches from head to tail. Marsh harriers glide over reed beds and open farmland to hunt. They are fearsome predators that eat birds, small mammals and reptiles.

◄ DOWN IN THE JUNGLE

The harpy eagle lives in the dense forests and jungles of Central and South America. It is an awesome predator, picking animals as big as sloths and monkeys from the trees, as well as birds such as parrots. Harpy eagles grow up to 3 feet from head to tail. They have huge talons that can grip heavy prey.

▲ DAYLIGHT OWL

Hawk owls live mainly in the forests of the far north, where there is permanent daylight in the summer. They usually sit on a perch and dart out to catch prey.

▼ EAGLE AT SEA

The white-bellied sea eagle lives high on the clifftops of an island in Indonesia, Southeast Asia. Like other sea eagles, it takes fish from both coastal and inland waters and also feeds on carrion. This eagle will even eat poisonous sea snakes.

▲ FLEET FLIER

The sparrowhawk is found in the woodlands of Europe and Asia. It flies swiftly and close to the ground, using the dense vegetation as cover. However, it sometimes hunts like a peregrine, circling high and then diving steeply at its prey.

Horses of the World

There are no truly wild horses any more, but feral herds are found all over the world. Feral horses are the descendants of tame horses that escaped from people. They run wild without any human interference. Semi-wild horses also run free, although these horses are owned by people and are sometimes rounded up to be tamed. Horses can live in many different habitats because their main food, grass, grows in most open areas.

The relatives of horses— asses and zebras—are less widespread. Zebras are found only in Africa, south of the Sahara Desert. Wild asses live in scattered areas of eastern Africa and Asia. Many species of wild ass and zebra are now threatened with extinction.

NORTH AMERICA

1 8

2

3

SOUTH AMERICA

4

◄ OUTBACK
Australia has the largest number of feral horses in the world. They are known as brumbies and can be found in a wide range of habitats throughout Australia. They run wild over dry plains, wetlands, grasslands and in the mountains.

▼ SOUTH AMERICA
These feral horses live in the Falkland Islands, near Argentina. Their home is one of moorland, sand dunes and rocks.

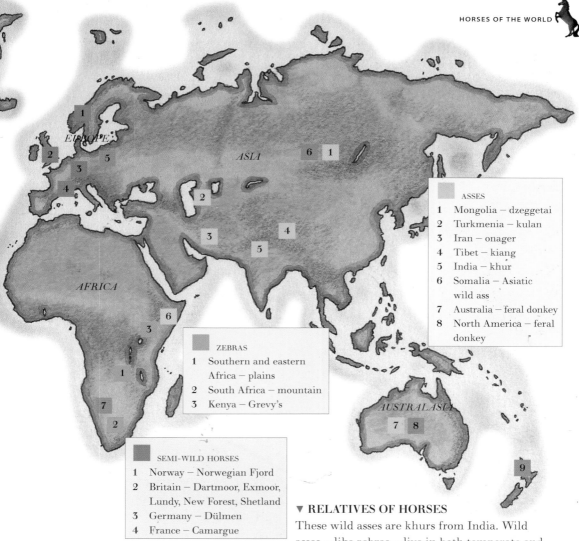

EUROPE

ASIA

AFRICA

AUSTRALASIA

ASSES

1 Mongolia – dzeggetai
2 Turkmenia – kulan
3 Iran – onager
4 Tibet – kiang
5 India – khur
6 Somalia – Asiatic
   wild ass
7 Australia – feral donkey
8 North America – feral
   donkey

ZEBRAS

1 Southern and eastern
   Africa – plains
2 South Africa – mountain
3 Kenya – Grevy's

SEMI-WILD HORSES

1 Norway – Norwegian Fjord
2 Britain – Dartmoor, Exmoor,
   Lundy, New Forest, Shetland
3 Germany – Dülmen
4 France – Camargue

FERAL HORSES

1 Western North America – mustang
2 Sable Island, Canada – Sable Island
3 Assateague Island, USA – Assateague,
   Chincoteague
4 Argentina – Criollo
5 Poland – tarpan
6 Mongolia – Przewalski
7 Namibia – Namib Desert
8 Australia – brumby
9 New Zealand – Kaimanawa

▼ RELATIVES OF HORSES

These wild asses are khurs from India. Wild
asses—like zebras—live in both temperate and
dry, tropical regions. Both species roam in small
herds over open landscapes such as the savannas of
Africa and the dry, rocky scrubland of Asia.

Tough Horses

WATCH THEM PLAY
Scenes such as these horses at play can be enjoyed by tourists. A blind has been set up so that people can watch the Namib Desert horses. Conservationists are divided about the horses. Some want them protected, while others want to remove them so that they do not damage the fragile desert environment.

DRINKING IN THE DESERT
Water is scarce in the desert and the horses must trek many miles to drink. These horses have started to adapt to their desert life and they are smaller than the horses from which they descended. They also urinate less, and can go without water for up to five days.

There is just one population of feral horses that has learned to survive in the desert. These horses have lived in the Namib Desert, in southwestern Africa, for over 80 years. Their ancestors were brought to Namibia by European settlers, but escaped from their owners or were released into the wild.

Horses are not natural desert dwellers, and so they have not evolved the many special features that enable other animals to thrive in hot, dry climates. The Namib horses came close to extinction in the 1970s. Just in time, people created a water supply especially for the horses. This was enough to tip the balance towards survival. Today there are about 150 horses living in the Namib Desert—one of only two or three feral groups in Africa.

of the Desert

UPS AND DOWNS OF DESERT LIFE

Namib Desert horses have survived against all odds. They live alongside specialized desert animals such as the gemsbok, ostrich and springbok.

THE NEW GENERATION

The horses breed when the rains come and food is relatively plentiful. There are few Namib horses, and they can only breed with each other because the horses live so far away from other herds. Scientists are interested in studying the effects of such inbreeding.

SAND BATHING

Horses keep their coats in good condition by rolling in sand. Namib horses are relatively free of parasites because of their isolation in a hot, dry desert. This unique environment is useful to scientists trying to understand how animals cope with extreme climate change.

ESSENTIAL RAIN

The Namib horses are thin for most of their lives, but they grow fatter and the population swells in years of good rains. The sudden growth of desert plants provides them with an instant food bonanza.

Elephant Habitats

The two species of elephant, African and Asian elephants, are divided into smaller groups called subspecies. The subspecies each look a little different from one another and are named after their habitats. Africa has three subspecies—the bush elephant of the open grasslands, the forest elephant of western and central Africa, and the desert elephant of Namibia. The main subspecies throughout South-east Asia is the Indian elephant. Asia is also home to two other subspecies, the Sumatran and Sri Lankan elephants.

▲ IN A SUMATRAN SWAMP
Sumatran elephants wade into swamps to find juicy grasses to feast on. They are the smallest of the Asian subspecies. These elephants are also the lightest in colour, and have fewer pink patches than the other Asian subspecies.

ASIAN GIANT ▶
The rare Sri Lankan elephant is the biggest and darkest of the three Asian subspecies.

Did you know? The desert elephant is the tallest elephant in the world, at over thirteen feet high.

forest elephant
(Loxodonta africana cyclotis)

◀ ADAPTED FOR THE FORESTS
The forest elephant is the smallest African subspecies, and its size enables it to move easily through the trees. Elephants lose heat through their ears, so it is no surprise that this species, living in the cooler forests, has smaller ears than other elephants.

◄ SURVIVAL IN THE DESERT
The hot, dry deserts of Namibia in southwestern Africa are home to the rare desert elephant. This subspecies is very closely related to the African bush elephant, but it has longer legs. Desert elephants have to walk long distances to find food and water. Scientists think that this is why they have longer legs than any other subspecies.

ELEPHANT WORLD ►
African elephants live in a broad band across central and southern Africa. They became extinct in North Africa around AD300. Today, Asian elephants live in hilly or mountainous areas of India, Sri Lanka, Southeast Asia, Malaysia, Indonesia and southern China. In the past, they roamed all across Asia.

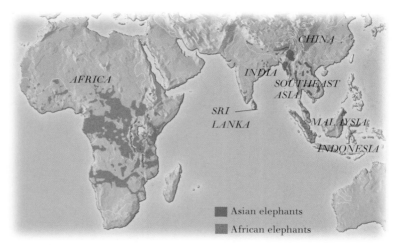

■ Asian elephants
■ African elephants

▲ IN THE SAVANNA
African bush elephants live in savanna (areas of grassland with scattered trees). Some, however, live in forests, marshes and even on mountains.

◄ SOLIDLY BUILT
The African bush elephant is bulkier and heavier than any other elephant. Like all elephants, its large size is a useful weapon against lions, tigers and other predators.

Indian Ocean

main road

Somawathiya
National Park

Minneriya Giritale
Nature Reserve

Trikonamadu
Nature Reserve

Floodplain
National Park

Mahaweli
Ganga River

main road

Wasgamuwa
National Park

protected areas   planned extension
to protected areas

▲ ANIMAL CORRIDORS

Much of Sri Lanka is used for agriculture, so elephants tend to live in protected nature reserves. They move between the regions along special corridors of land, in the same way that people travel between cities along highways.

Roaming Elephants

Like horses, elephants are constantly on the move, searching for food. They travel about 15 miles a day, ranging over a wide area.

Twice a year, elephants make long migrations to a new area to search for food and water. They gather in large groups for these journeys. The elephants follow the same paths year after year as each generation of elephants learns the route. Today, elephants have been squeezed into smaller areas as human beings take up more and more land. As a result, their migrations are much shorter than they used to be, although they may still walk for hundreds of miles.

ELEPHANT RAIDERS ▶

This corn field on the island of Sumatra lies on a traditional migration route. Elephants can do a lot of damage to crops, and farmers try to scare them away.

◀ ELEPHANT WELLS

During times of drought, elephants may dig holes in dry stream beds. They use their trunks, tusks and feet to reach water hidden under the ground. Elephants need to drink 75–95 quarts of water each day. They have been known to travel distances of up to 20 miles to reach a tiny patch of rainfall. Elephant wells can be lifesavers for other wildlife that come to drink the water after the elephants have gone.

LONG JOURNEYS ▶
African elephants on the savanna may wander over an area of more than 1,800 square miles. The extent of their migrations depends on the weather and other conditions. Asian elephants living in forests migrate over smaller areas of 60–200 square miles.

◀ WATCHING FROM ABOVE
Migrating elephants can be followed by airplane in open country. Little or no rain falls during the dry season and the elephants tend to group together in places where water is available. The thirsty animals usually mill around a river valley or a swamp. In rainy seasons, elephants spread out over a wider area.

◀ PUSHING THROUGH
Elephants will try anything to find a way through farmers' fences. They can use their tusks to break electric fence wires and even drop large rocks or logs on top of fences.

KEEPING TRACK ▶
Scientists in Africa put a radio collar on an elephant. This device tracks the animal's movements without disturbing its natural behavior.

Where Bears Live

Most types of habitat are home to a species of bear. Bears live in temperate and tropical forests, on mountain slopes, scrub desert and tropical grasslands, and on the Arctic tundra. Each species, however, has its own preferred environment. The polar bear, for example, inhabits the lands and sea ice bordering the Arctic Ocean. It favors shoreline areas where the ice breaks up as this is where its main food source, seals, gather. Most other bears are less fussy about what they eat, and have the uncanny ability to turn up wherever food is abundant. However, many of the wilderness areas where bears live are threatened. Every year, more land is cultivated for farmland and forests all over the world are cut down.

▲ IN THE BAMBOO FORESTS
The giant panda is restricted to areas of abundant bamboo forest. It was once much more widespread across eastern Asia, but now survives in just three provinces of western China – Gansu, Shanxi and Sichuan.

▼ MOUNTAIN BEAR
The spectacled bear of South America feeds on fruit and juicy leaves. It is found in humid forests as well as on open grassland and rocky areas high in the Andes Mountains.

spectacled bear
(Tremarctos ornatus)

▲ THE ADAPTABLE BROWN
The brown bear is the most widespread of all bears. It is found in Europe and the Middle East, and across northern Asia to Japan. North American brown bears, called Grizzly Bears, live in Alaska and the Rockies.

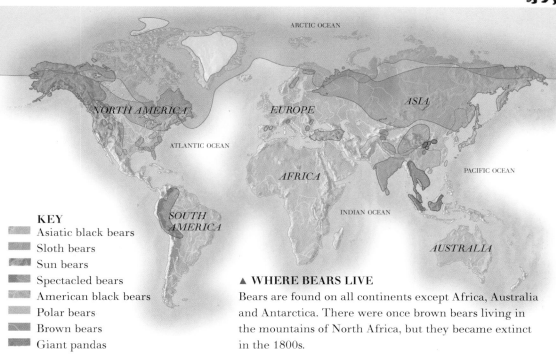

KEY
- Asiatic black bears
- Sloth bears
- Sun bears
- Spectacled bears
- American black bears
- Polar bears
- Brown bears
- Giant pandas

▲ WHERE BEARS LIVE

Bears are found on all continents except Africa, Australia and Antarctica. There were once brown bears living in the mountains of North Africa, but they became extinct in the 1800s.

▲ MOUNTAIN BLACK

The Asiatic black bear lives in mountainous regions. Although related to the American black bear, Asiatic bears are smaller, perhaps because the conditions they live in are harsher.

▲ LIFE IN THE FOREST

The sloth bear lives in dense, dry forests in India and Sri Lanka. It feeds mostly at night, on leaves and fruits on the forest floor. During the day, the bear rests in a tree where it is surprisingly well camouflaged. Sloth bears are agile climbers, gripping the trees with their long claws.

45

Pandas in

Giant pandas live in the bamboo forests of western China. For most of the year, the panda's distinctive black and white coats stand out clearly among the greenery. But in winter, the bears become difficult to see in the snow. Some scientists believe that pandas developed their coat as a camouflage at some point in their history. They have had no reason to perfect it because there are few large predators in the areas where pandas live.

Although giant pandas are very rare—there are probably only a few hundred left in the wild—they are fairly safe as long as people do not destroy their forest homes. Habitat destruction is the largest threat to pandas.

FINDING FOOD

Bamboo forms over 99 percent of pandas' diets, although they do supplement their diet with meat when they can get it. Pandas catch rats and beetles in the bamboo, and have been known to scavenge at leopard kills. But easy prey is scarce and pandas make clumsy hunters. The abundant bamboo makes for easier picking.

THIRSTY WORK

Most of the water a panda needs comes from bamboo. If a bear is thirsty, it scoops out a hollow by a stream and drinks as much as it can. The giant panda is most active in the early morning and late afternoon. It spends 16 or more hours a day feeding.

the Bamboo Forest

ESSENTIAL FOOD

Bamboo is plentiful and easy for the bears to harvest, but digesting it is hard work. This is because the panda's digestive system is more characteristic of a carnivore. Pandas eat huge quantities of bamboo every day in order to keep going. It takes a long time for animals to evolve the perfect body to suit a new habitat.

FEEDING ALL YEAR

Even in the coldest months, bamboo is green and nutritious so the panda has a continuous supply of food. Unlike some other bears, whose food is scarce at certain times, the panda remains active throughout the winter. A thick fur coat protects it from the snow and the cold.

GOOD GRIP

A panda's front paws are specially adapted to manipulate bamboo. The wrist bones have become elongated to create a "thumb." A panda usually feeds sitting upright on its haunches. This leaves its forelegs free to handle the bamboo stalks.

Polar Bears

The polar bear is perfectly adapted to life in the Arctic, where winter temperatures can drop to -60°F. Beneath its skin lies a thick layer of fat. The bear's entire body, including the soles of the feet, is covered in insulating fur made up of thick hairs with a woolly underfur. Each hair is not actually white, but translucent and hollow. It acts like a tiny greenhouse, allowing light and heat from the sun to pass through, trapping the warm air. Sometimes, for example in zoos, the hairs are invaded by tiny algae and the polar bear's coat has a green tinge. In the wild, the fur often appears yellow, the result of oil stains from its seal prey. Beneath the fur the skin is black, which absorbs heat. This excellent insulation keeps the polar bear's body at a constant 98.6°F.

Respect for the Ice Bear
The polar bear is the most powerful spirit in Arctic cultures. The Inuit believe that a polar bear has a soul. It will only allow itself to be killed if the hunter treats it properly after death. It is forbidden to hunt another bear too soon. Time must be left for the bear's soul to return to its family. Some Inuit offer a dead male bear a miniature bow and arrow, and a female bear a needle holder.

◄ SEA-GOING BEAR
Polar bears are excellent swimmers. They must swim frequently because their icy world is unpredictable. In winter, the Arctic Ocean freezes over. But with the arrival of storms and warmer weather the ice breaks up. Then the bear must swim between ice floes in search of seals. The thick layer of fat below the skin and dense, insulating fur allow a polar bear to swim in the coldest seas without suffering. In such cold water, a human being would be dead in a few minutes.

▲ COOLING DOWN IN THE ARCTIC

Polar bears are so well insulated they are in danger of overheating on warm days. To keep cool, they lie flat out on the ice. At other times they lie on their backs with their feet in the air.

▲ BEAR SLUMBERS

A polar bear, like a human, sleeps for seven or eight hours at a time. This helps the polar bear to conserve energy and heat. Polar bears are not at risk of attack when they are sleeping, so they do not have to hide like other animals. Most often, polar bears find a sheltered area to protect them from the cold winds that blow across the Arctic.

▲ PROTECTED FROM THE COLD

The insulating fur and fat of a polar bear are so efficient that little heat is lost. In fact, if a scientist were to look at a polar bear with an infrared camera (which detects heat given off by the body), only the bear's nose and eyes would be visible.

CHANGING ENVIRONMENT ▶

Polar bears are most active at the start of the day. During summer, when the ice melts and retreats, bears may be prevented from hunting seals. Then they rest, living off their fat reserves and eating berries.

Cats of the Savanna

Large areas of Africa are covered with grasslands called savannas. Rain falls at certain times of the year, but there is not enough water for forests to grow. The tall grasses provide food for huge herds of antelope, zebra and other grazing animals. These in turn are eaten by many predators, which use various methods to catch the fast-moving prey. The big cats are among the most successful predators on the savannas. Lions, leopards and cheetahs all make their home on the African savanna, together with several smaller cats such as the serval. Similar grasslands in South America are home to the powerful jaguar.

▲ CAMOUFLAGE CAT
A lion strolls through the African savanna, its sandy coloring perfectly matching its habitat. When a lion hunts, it uses the cover of grass to hide from its quarry. It must creep up fairly close without being spotted.

This map shows where the world's tropical grasslands are located. The largest region of savanna is in Africa.

Did you know? Cats sleep for longer than most other animals. Lions sleep for 20 hours a day.

◄ ON THE LOOKOUT
Cheetahs are perfectly adapted for life on the plains. Here, a cheetah stands on the top of a small mound on the Kenyan savanna. It is searching for prey with its excellent eyesight. Once it spots a vulnerable animal, it races over the open, flat terrain to catch its victim. Cheetahs are the fastest of all land mammals. They can reach speeds of 70 miles per hour.

◄ VIEW FROM A BRANCH

Leopards like to live in areas of grassland where there are trees. Here they can sleep hidden during the heat of the day. They avoid the insects that live in the grass below and can enjoy the afternoon breeze. Leopards also prefer to eat in a tree, out of the reach of scavengers.

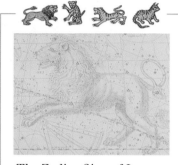

The Zodiac Sign of Leo
People born between July 24 and August 23 are born under the astrological sign of Leo (the lion). They are said to be brave, strong and proud, just like lions.

▲ AT THE WATER HOLE

During the dry season in the African savanna, many grazing animals gather near water holes to drink. Giraffes, Thomson's gazelles and zebras are shown here. Lions congregate around the water holes, not only to drink, but also to catch prey unawares. Their favorite prey animals are antelope, zebra and warthog, but they also eat young giraffes and buffalo.

SPEEDY SERVAL ►

Servals are small cats that live all over the African savanna. They like to live near water where there are bushes to hide in. The servals' long legs enable them to leap over tall grass when they hunt small rodents. They also climb well and hunt birds. With their long legs, servals can run quickly over short distances and so can easily escape from predators.

Forest Cats

Dense, wet rainforests are home to many insects that are eaten by birds, snakes, frogs and small mammals. In turn, these animals provide a feast for big cats. Tigers, jaguars, leopards and clouded leopards all live in rainforests, as do smaller cats including ocelots and margays. Their striped or spotted coats provide good camouflage. Forest cats hunt on the ground and in trees. They usually rest during the day and hunt at night, tracking down their prey using their superb hearing and eyesight.

▲ UP IN THE CLOUDS

The clouded leopard is a shy and rarely seen Asian big cat. It lives in forests from Nepal to Borneo, spending most of its time in the trees. Clouded leopards are about three feet long with an equally long tail, and weigh about 65 pounds. They are smaller than true leopards and they can move around easily in the trees. Clouded leopards are perfectly built for climbing, with a long, bushy tail for balance and flexible ankle joints.

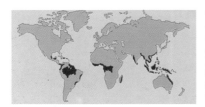

This map shows where the world's tropical rainforests are located. They lie in a band on either side of the Equator.

▼ OUT OF REACH

Leopards live in Africa and southern Asia in all kinds of habitat, from rainforest to dry grassland. They are great climbers and often drag their prey high into trees where they can be safe from thieving hyenas.

Did you know? The jaguar was the symbol of the sun for the Maya of Central America.

▲ TAKING ADVANTAGE OF THE WATER
A tiger walks stealthily into a jungle pool
on the island of Sumatra. Tigers are good
swimmers, and a forest pool is a good place to
hunt as well as to cool off from the tropical
heat. Tigers often hide the carcasses of their
prey in water or in the dense undergrowth.

▲ TOP CAT
Margays live in the tropical forests of Central
and South America. They are the best of all
cat climbers, with broad, soft feet and
exceptionally flexible ankles and hind legs.
They feed largely on birds and so need to be
good at moving around in the tops of trees.

▲ LOSS OF HABITAT
Jaguars can be found all over South and Central
America but they prefer thick forests. They are
threatened by over-hunting and the destruction
of their forest habitat.

◄ LOST IN THE DARK
Forest leopards and
jaguars are darker than
their grassland cousins.
Some are even black. The
dark color helps them to
virtually disappear in the
shadows of their forest habitat.

▲ A TURTLE TREAT
A jaguar catches a river turtle in a pool. Jaguars
are such good swimmers that they hunt some of
their prey in water. They love to eat fish and
turtles. Their jaws are powerful enough to crack
open a turtle's shell like a nut. They have also
been known to kill caimans, a type of crocodile.

53

Mountain Cats

To live in the mountains, cats need to be hardy and excellent rock climbers. They also have to cope with high altitudes where the air is thin and there is less oxygen to breathe. Mountain climates are harsh, and the weather can change very quickly. To survive, mountain cats need to use their wits and to know where to find shelter. They mate so that their cubs are born in the spring. This is to ensure that they will be almost grown by the time winter closes in. Big cats that live in the mountains include leopards and the rare snow leopard. Small cats include the puma, mountain cat, bobcat and lynx.

▲ **SOUTH AMERICAN CAT**
The Andean mountain cat is a secretive, shy creature and seldom seen. It is about 20 inches long and has soft, fine fur. It lives in the high Andes mountains of Chile, Argentina, Peru and Bolivia. This cat is found at altitudes of up to 16,000 feet above sea level.

This map shows the world's major mountain ranges. The puma, lynx and mountain cat live in the Americas. Lynx also live in Europe and Asia, while the snow leopard lives in Asia.

◄ **SURVEYING THE SLOPES**
A puma, sometimes known as a mountain lion, keeps watch over its vast territory. Male pumas can grow to 7 feet long, and weigh 225 pounds. They are good at jumping and can easily leap 15 feet onto a high rock or into a tree. Pumas are found over a wide area, from Canada to the very tip of South America in Chile. They live along the foothills of mountains, in forests on mountain slopes and all the way up to 15,000 feet above sea level. Depending on where they live, pumas will eat porcupines, deer, beavers, hares and armadillos.

IN THE COLD ▶
Lynx live in mountainous regions of Europe, Asia and North America. They have unusually short tails and tufted ears. Lynx are well designed to live in very cold places. In winter they grow an especially long coat, which is light colored so that they are well camouflaged in the snow.

◀ MOUNTAIN CHASE
A snowshoe hare darts this way and that to shake off a puma. To catch the hare, the puma makes full use of its flexible back and its long balancing tail. Pumas hunt by day as well as by night.

KING OF THE MOUNTAINS ▶
The snow leopard is one of the rarest big cats, found only in the Himalaya and Altai mountains of central Asia. It can live at altitudes of 20,000 feet, the highest of any wild cat. Snow leopards feed on wild goats, hares and marmots. Their bodies measure just over 3 feet long, with tails that are almost as long. They wrap their bushy tails around themselves to keep warm when they are sleeping. Snow leopards are agile jumpers and are said to be able to leap a gap of 50 feet. Their long tails help them to balance as they jump.

Did you know? Snow leopards are well adapted to the cold – even their feet are covered with fur.

▲ JACKAL ON ALERT
A side-striped jackal keeps a wary lookout for danger. In Africa, the three different kinds of jackal are found in different types of terrain. Side-striped jackals keep mostly to woods and swampy areas. Golden and black-backed jackals live in more open countryside.

Forest-living Wolves and Wild Dogs

Trees cover much of the world. Canada, Russia and northern Europe have many dense evergreen forests. Warmer, temperate regions contain broad-leaved woodlands. Nearer the Equator, tropical rainforests grow. In all of these areas, wolves or other species of wild dogs can be found.

Forests provide a plentiful supply of prey and dense undergrowth in which to hide and stalk. Wolves tend to live in northern regions, where large game such as deer abound. Temperate forests in Asia provide a home for the raccoon dog. Bush dogs are one of the few wild dogs to live in the rainforest. It is harder for wild dogs to survive in tropical rainforests, because most of the small prey animals live out of reach in the treetops.

◄ HIDDEN HUNTERS
In dark pine forests and dappled broad-leaved woodlands, the grey or blackish coats of wolves blend in with the shadows. This helps them to sneak up on moose, deer and other forest prey. In Arctic regions, wolves can have almost white coats, an effective camouflage in the snow.

◄ SOUND SLEEPERS

Raccoon dogs live in thickly wooded river valleys in eastern Asia. They are the only species of dog that hibernates in winter. In autumn, raccoon dogs gorge themselves on fruit and meat to put on a thick layer of fat. Then they retreat to their burrows and sleep through the harsh winter.

JUNGLE PACK ►

This wild dog is called a dhole. Packs of dholes hunt deer in the dense forests in Southeast Asia. They call to one another to surround their prey as it moves through the jungle. The pack will guard its kills against bears, tigers and scavengers.

◄ RODENTS BEWARE

Bush dogs make their home in the dense rainforests and marshlands of South America. They live close to rivers and streams, where they find plenty of animals to eat. Their main prey are aquatic rodents such as pacas and agoutis. Bush dogs will even plunge into the water to hunt capybaras—the world's largest rodents, at 4½ feet long.

A SCARCE BREED ►

A wolf surveys the snowy landscape in the Abruzzo region of central Italy. Wolves are common in remote forests in Canada and Russia, but in western Europe they are scarce. They survive in small pockets of wilderness, hiding in the hills by day and creeping down to villages to steal scraps at night.

Wild Dogs of Desert and Grassland

Wild dogs inhabit open country, as well as forests. Deserts are one of the harshest environments for wild dogs. In these barren places, the sun beats down mercilessly by day, but at night the temperature plummets. Coyotes, dingoes and foxes survive in these barren places. They can live for long periods with little water, and derive most of the liquid they need from their food. Desert foxes keep cool during the hot days by hiding under rocks or in dark burrows, emerging to hunt only at night.

Many species of wild dog live on the world's grasslands, including African hunting dogs, maned wolves and jackals.

▲ CHANGE OF COLOR
Wolves are found in deserts and dry areas in Mexico, Iran and Arabia. With little vegetation to provide cover, they stalk prey by hiding behind boulders or rocky outcrops. Desert wolves often have pale or sandy fur, to blend in with their surroundings.

▲ GIVING OFF HEAT
This jackal lives in the desert. Its large ears contain a network of fine veins. Blood flowing through these veins gives off heat, keeping the animal cool.

◄ HUNTERS OF THE OUTBACK
A pair of dingoes wait at a rabbit warren. Dingoes are descended from domestic dogs, but have lived wild in central Australia for more than 8,000 years. Their reddish-brown coats, with paler fur on their legs and bellies, are perfect desert camouflage.

▲ ADAPTING TO THE WILD

Feral dogs are the descendants of
domestic dogs that have become wild.
In Asia they are known as pariah
(outcast) dogs. Feral dogs are very
adaptable and change their behavior
to suit any situation. In India, pariah
dogs hang around villages and sneak
in to scavenge scraps.

▲ AVOIDING THE HEAT

A pack of African hunting dogs tears a carcass apart.
These dogs live on the open grasslands of Africa, which
have scorching daytime temperatures. The dogs tend
to hunt in the early morning or late evening, when it
is cooler, to avoid overheating. Gazelles and zebras are
their main prey.

▲ SLY MARSHLAND HUNTER

A maned wolf hunts in Argentinian marshland. Its long legs
help it to see over the tall grass, but it is not a fast runner.
It also lacks the stamina needed to chase prey over great
distances. Instead, it stalks animals such as rodents by slowly
sneaking up on them before making a sudden pounce.

The Jackal-headed God

*In ancient Egypt, Anubis, the
god of the dead, was shown
with a human body and the
head of a jackal. This god was
believed to be responsible for
the process of embalming,
which preserved the bodies of
the dead. Anubis often appears
in wall paintings and sculptures
found in burial places. Here he
is shown embalming the body
of an Egyptian king.*

Forest Apes

There are five species of apes: chimpanzees, bonobos, gorillas, gibbons and orangutans. They all live in Africa or Southeast Asia. Most apes inhabit tropical rainforests, but chimpanzees can be found in more open, deciduous woodlands and in wooded grasslands, and some gorillas prefer mountain forests with their lush vegetation and misty atmosphere. Gibbons sometimes live in deciduous forests, too.

All the apes used to be more widespread, but they are being gradually squeezed into smaller and smaller areas as people hunt them and destroy their habitats.

▲ VANISHING APE
In the dark and dappled rainforest where orangutans live, their shaggy, orange hair blends in with the tangle of forest plants. This makes them surprisingly difficult to see.

▶ FOREST DETECTIVES
It is often hard for scientists to watch gorillas in their wooded habitats. Instead, they study the signs left behind by the gorillas as they move about the forest.

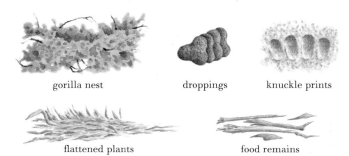

gorilla nest   droppings   knuckle prints

flattened plants   food remains

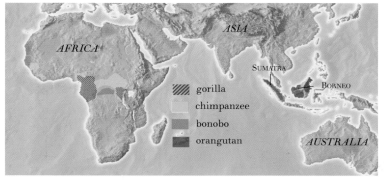

◀ WHERE APES LIVE
Gorillas, chimpanzees and bonobos live in Africa and orangutans live only on the islands of Borneo and Sumatra. However, orangutans once lived in parts of mainland Southeast Asia. Some people believe that they were hunted out by poachers.

ASIA
AFRICA
SUMATRA
BORNEO
AUSTRALIA

gorilla
chimpanzee
bonobo
orangutan

▲ LOCAL ROUTE MAP

Chimpanzees travel around their own neighborhoods on the ground, following a network of paths. They use a mental map in their heads to decide where to go. Each day they work out where to get a good meal, climbing trees to find fruit and leaves, or to chase prey.

▲ TREETOP HABITAT

Gibbons are totally at home in the tops of the trees and hardly ever go down to the ground. They are the only apes that do not build nests. Gibbons sleep sitting up in the forks of branches, resting on tough sitting pads. These pads act like built-in cushions for the gibbon.

▼ MAKING A COSY NEST

This chimpanzee is making a nest to sleep in. Every night, adult apes (apart from gibbons) make nests in the trees or on the ground. They bend and weave together leafy branches and pile more leaves and branches on top. This makes a warm, springy nest to keep out the cold.

▲ MOUNTAIN HOMES

Dense, misty forests up to about 11,000 feet above sea level are the home of mountain gorillas. At night, the temperature sometimes drops to below freezing but the long hair of the gorillas helps them to keep warm.

chimpanzee
(Pan troglodytes)

Lowland and

It's 6.30 in the morning. A group of mountain gorillas is waking up. They are hungry after their night-time fast and reach out to pick a leafy breakfast in bed. Then the gorillas move off through the forest, feeding as they go. After a morning spent munching plants, they build day nests on the ground and take a rest for a couple of hours. This gives them time to digest their food and socialize. These gorillas live amid the beautiful and misty volcanic Virunga Mountains in Africa. They have lowland cousins who live in the tropical rainforests of eastern and western Central Africa.

CAREFUL CLIMBERS
Adult gorillas climb with great care and feel most secure when all four limbs are in contact with a branch. Young gorillas (*above*) are lighter and often play by hanging from a branch or swinging from tree to tree.

MOUNTAIN REFUGE
In 1925, the home of the mountain gorilla on the slopes of the Virunga volcanoes was declared Africa's first national park. The word virunga comes from a local expression meaning 'isolated mountains that reach the clouds.' The Virunga Mountains include both active and dormant volcanoes, but the gorillas live only on the dormant volcanoes.

SNACK IN A SWAMP
Traveling through the Odzala Forest at about 2–2½ miles per hour, these western lowland gorillas feed in a swampy glade. Like all gorillas, they walk on all fours.

Mountain Gorillas

GORILLA CHAMPION
From her hut on Mount Visoke, Dian Fossey devoted herself to studying and protecting mountain gorillas. She began her work in 1967, winning the trust of the gorillas, studying their family relationships and making discoveries about their behavior.

LIVING IN THE MIST
Mists often swirl around the forests where the mountain gorillas live, so they are called cloud forests. Mosses and lichens grow well in the cool, damp air, and hang on the branches like untidy green hair.

LOWLAND FORESTS
Eastern lowland gorillas live in the lowland rainforests of eastern Congo. It is more difficult for people to study lowland gorillas because the rainforests are less open than the mountain gorillas' habitat.

FOOD FOR FREE
On the rainy slopes where they live, the mountain gorillas have a wide variety of food, such as wild celery, bedstraw, bamboo shoots, thistles, brambles and nettles.

Mammals of the Open Sea

Whales and dolphins are mammals. Like all mammals, they breathe air and feed their young on milk. Their ancestors evolved on land, and so whales and dolphins have had to make many adaptations to live in a watery environment. They have a layer of fatty blubber beneath their ·skin to keep them warm, and can hold their breath for many minutes before needing to surface.

Whales and dolphins are found in all the world's oceans. Each species has a unique survival strategy to take advantage of its habitat.

◄ OCEAN WANDERER
Humpback whales migrate vast distances to find the perfect conditions for hunting and breeding.

▲ IN THE MUD
Like other dolphins that live in rivers rather than the sea, the Amazon river dolphin has a long jaw, or beak, to help it catch its prey. Its flexible neck helps it to maneuver around submerged trees and tangled vegetation in the muddy waters where it lives.

◄ WORLDWIDE KILLER
Among ice floes in the Arctic Ocean, a killer whale hunts for prey. Killer whales are found in all the oceans of the world. They live in coastal areas but may venture out to the open ocean. They also swim close to the shore, and may deliberately run aground to snatch a seal as their prey before letting the next wave wash them back to sea.

FAR NORTH ▶
A group of beluga whales swims in Hudson Bay, Canada. Belugas live around coasts in the far north of the world. In winter they hunt for fish under the pack ice in the Arctic. Belugas have a thick layer of blubber that protects them from the cold.

◀ WARM WATERS
These melon-headed whales prefer warm waters and are found in subtropical and tropical regions in both the northern and southern hemispheres. Melon-headed whales feed on a whole range of fish and squid, which they generally catch in deep water, well away from land.

WIDE RANGER ▶
The bottlenose dolphin is one of the most wide-ranging dolphin species, found in temperate and tropical waters in both the northern and southern hemispheres. It is also found in enclosed seas such as the Mediterranean and Red seas. When bottlenose dolphins migrate to warmer areas, they lose weight. When they return to colder climes, their blubber increases again to protect them against the cold.

Shark Habitats

Each one of the world's oceans and seas is home to at least one species of shark. Often there are many species, living at different depths and hunting different prey. Some sharks, like bull sharks, even swim in rivers and lakes. Whale, reef and nurse sharks are all tropical species that prefer warm waters. Temperate-water sharks, such as the mako, horn and basking sharks, live in water with a temperature of 50–70°F. Cold-water sharks often live in deep water. The Portuguese shark, frilled shark, and goblin shark are all cold-water sharks. A few species will swim in extremely cold waters, such as the Greenland shark which lives around the Arctic Circle.

NORTH
AMERICA

ATLAN
OCEAN

PACIFIC OCEAN

SOUTH
AMERICA

▶ SWIMMING POOLS
This map shows the main parts of the world's seas in which different kinds of sharks live. The key beneath the map shows which sharks live where.

LOOKING FOR FOOD ▶
The oceanic whitetip shark lives in tropical and subtropical waters. It is one of the first sharks to appear at shipwrecks, perhaps because shipwrecks shelter lots of other fish for the whitetip to eat.

◀ ISLAND LIVING
The Galapagos shark swims in the waters of the Galapagos Islands, on the Equator. It also swims around other tropical islands in the Pacific, Atlantic and Indian oceans.

KEY

whale shark

basking shark

bull shark

tiger shark

whitetip shark

Greenland shark

great white shark

◀ UNDER THE ICE

The Greenland shark lives in deep water, and is the only shark known to survive under polar ice in the North Atlantic. It has a luminous parasite attached to each eye that attracts prey to the area around its mouth.

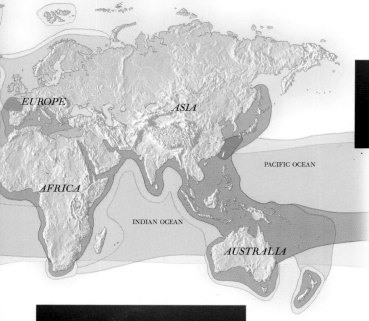

EUROPE

ASIA

AFRICA

PACIFIC OCEAN

INDIAN OCEAN

AUSTRALIA

▲ FEARSOME KILLER

The great white shark lives in temperate, tropical and sub-tropical seas. It grows to over 20 feet long and is the largest hunting fish in the seas. Its powerful jaws can bite a fully grown elephant seal (which is about 13 feet long) in half. It has strong, triangular teeth that can slice through flesh, blubber and even bone.

▲ TIGER OF THE SEAS

The tiger shark has a long, rounded shape, typical of hunting sharks. It swims mainly in tropical and warm temperate waters, both in the open ocean, and close to shore.

◀ REEF PATROL

The blacktip reef shark patrols reefs in the Indian and Pacific oceans. It also lives in shallow waters in the Red Sea and the Mediterranean, as far west as the waters off Tunisia, in North Africa.

67

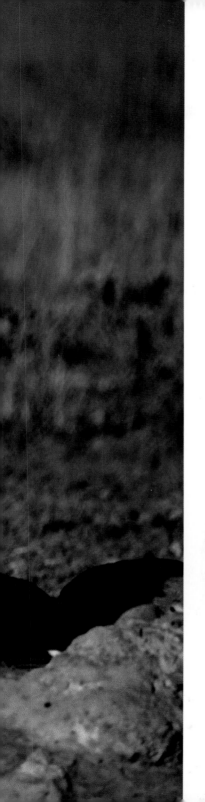

The Hunt for Food

There are fundamental physical differences between animals that eat meat and those that feed on plants. This section focuses on the special adaptations that animals have made in order to take advantage of one particular food, and it explores their similarities and differences.

The Diet of Animals

All living things need food of some kind or another. Food provides them with the energy needed to move about and to power all of life's other activities. Food also provides the "building blocks" needed for growth. Plants use the energy in sunlight to make their own food by a process called photosynthesis, but animals all have to find and eat "ready-made" food in the form of plants or other animals. Animals that feed on plants are called herbivores. Those that eat meat or flesh are called carnivores and those that regularly eat both plants and other animals are called omnivores. We are omnivores, and so are chimpanzees and most bears.

Pandas have given up regular hunting in favor of a diet of bamboo.

Sensing food

Herbivorous animals generally track down tasty foods by using their eyes and sense of smell. Nectar-seeking butterflies, for example, home in on flowers by picking up their colors and scents, and grazing mammals can smell fresh grass from many miles away. Carnivores use their eyes, their sense of smell and also their ears to find food. Many snakes track down their prey by flicking out their tongues to pick up traces of scent on the ground or in the air. Rattlesnakes have heat-sensitive pits on their snouts that tell them when warm-blooded prey is near. This is particularly useful at night. Hearing is also important for animals that hunt at night. Owls have excellent hearing as well as superb eyesight. Their ears pick up the slightest rustle in the grass below and enable the owls to home in on their prey with amazing accuracy. Soft-edged feathers enable the owls to fly very quietly, so the prey does not hear them coming.

Snakes use their senses to detect other animals and, instead of hunting, many snakes simply lie in wait for their prey to come to them.

To chase or to lie in wait?

Meat-eaters have two main ways of getting their
food. They can chase after their prey, or they can hide
and lie in wait for it. Wolves and other dogs are chasers,
often hunting in packs to catch prey much larger than
themselves. The chase can last for hours, with the dogs
taking turns at the front. Lions and other cats also chase
their prey, but their chases are much shorter. Leopards
sometimes lie in wait for their prey, often sitting on a
branch or a rock and dropping on anything that passes
beneath. Some crab spiders lurk in flowers and often
blend so well with the petals that they are very hard to
see. Insects visiting the flowers for a drink are quickly
grabbed by the spiders. Many spiders make sticky webs
to trap their prey but some rely on sensing the
vibrations when prey walk over or near their webs.

*Most big cats are only too happy to eat
someone else's meal and steal kills from
other animals whenever they can. Cheetahs
are an exception, and eat only animals they
have killed themselves.*

Teeth and claws

Most predators use their claws or teeth to catch and kill their prey. Cats, for
example, use their powerful claws to bring down their victims, and then kill
them either by biting through the neck or by gripping the throat until their
prey suffocates. Birds of prey usually use their talons to snatch and kill
their victims. The birds then use their hooked beaks to tear up the flesh,
although owls usually swallow their prey whole. Mammalian teeth vary with
the animals' diets. Grass-eaters have big grinding teeth to crush grass and
release as much of the goodness from it as possible. Meat-eaters
have sharp-edged cheek teeth for slicing through the flesh of
their prey. Insect jaws are on the outside of the body and they
cut or crush the food before pushing it into their mouth.
Bugs feed on liquids by piercing plants or other animals
with sharp, tubular beaks. Butterflies suck up nectar with
slender "drinking straws."

*Eagles attack with
their talons. They are
so long, sharp and
deeply curved that
one swipe is usually
enough to kill
their prey.*

All depend on plants

Whatever they eat, all
animals depend on plants for their food.
Lions eat zebras and antelopes but the
nutrition provided by the meat of these
grazing animals comes from their diet of
grass and other plants. Even sharks depend
on plants as the fish that they eat feed on
plants floating near the surface of the sea.

*A swallowtail butterfly using its
long tongue to suck up nectar.*

Insect Plant-eaters

Many insect species are herbivores (plant-eaters), including caterpillars, most bugs and some beetles. Different insects specialize in eating particular parts of plants—the leaves, buds, seeds, roots or bark. Many plant-eating insects become pests when they feed on cultivated plants or crops. Other pests nibble things that humans would not consider edible, such as clothes, carpets and wooden furniture.

Beetles and bugs do not always eat the same food throughout their lives. Rose chafer beetles, for example, nibble petals and pollen, but their larvae (young) feed on rotting wood. Some adult beetles and bugs do not feed at all. Instead, they put all their energy into finding a mate and reproducing.

▲ TUNNEL-BORERS
Female bark beetles lay their eggs under the tree's bark. When the young hatch, each one eats its way through the soft wood just under the bark, creating a long, narrow tunnel just wide enough to squeeze through.

squash bug
(Coreus marginatus)

Did you know? Wood boring beetle grubs may eat for 7 years before they reach full size.

◀ SQUASH-LOVERS
Squash bugs are named after their favorite food. The squash-plant family includes zucchini and pumpkins. This bug is about to pierce a zucchini flower bud and suck out its sap. Most squash bugs are green or brown. They feed on leaves, flowers and seeds. The insects are serious pests in North America.

▲ A PLAGUE OF APHIDS

Aphids are small, soft-bodied bugs. They use their sharp, beaklike mouths to pierce plant leaves and stems and suck out the life-giving sap that is found inside. Aphids reproduce so quickly in warm weather that they can cover a plant within a few hours—and suck it dry.

▲ BEETLE ATTACK

Colorado beetles are high on the list of dangerous insects in many countries. The beetles originally came from the western United States, where they ate the leaves of local plants. When European settlers came and cultivated potatoes, the beetles ate the crop and did great damage. Colorado beetles later spread to become a major pest in Europe, but are now controlled by pesticides.

▲ SCALY FEEDERS

Most female scale insects have neither legs nor wings, but they can be identified as bugs as they have sucking mouthparts (beetles have biting jaws). Scale insects are usually hidden under waxy or horny scales, as shown here. The insects are piercing the skin of a juicy melon and sucking its juices.

▲ THE EVIL WEEVIL

These grains of wheat have been infested by a type of beetle called the grain weevil. The adult weevils bore through the grain's hard case with their long snouts to reach the soft kernel inside. Females lay their eggs inside the kernels. Then, when the young hatch, they can feed in safety.

Beetle and Bug Attack

ground beetle
(Loricera pilicornis)

Some insects eat only vegetable matter, others are carnivores (meat-eaters). Some of the carnivorous species hunt and kill live prey, while others are scavengers and feed on dead animals. There are also parasitic insects that live on larger animals and eat their flesh or suck their blood without killing them. Most insect predators feed on insects of around their own size. Some, however, tackle larger game, such as frogs, fish, tadpoles, snails and worms. Insects are adapted in different ways to catch and overpower their prey.

All beetles have jaws, which are used by the carnivorous species to seize and crush or crunch up their victims. Bugs have jointed mouthparts made for sucking living victims' juices from their bodies.

▲ SPEEDY HUNTER

A ground beetle feeds on a juicy worm it has caught. Ground beetles are a large family of over 20,000 species. Many species cannot fly, hence their name. However, most ground beetles are fast runners. The beetle uses its speed to overtake a fleeing victim. Once trapped, the victim is firmly grabbed in the attacker's powerful jaws.

◄ GONE FISHING

Great diving beetles are fierce aquatic hunters. They hunt fish, tadpoles, newts and small creatures that live in ponds and streams. This beetle has caught a stickleback. It grabs the fish in its jaws, then injects it with digestive juices that begin to dissolve the fish's flesh. When the victim finally stops struggling and dies, the beetle begins to feed.

Famous Victim
Charles Darwin (1809–1882), the British naturalist who first developed the theory of evolution, is thought by some to have been bitten by a South American assassin bug. Darwin had gone to South America to study wildlife. On his return to Britain, he fell victim to a mysterious illness, which weakened him for the rest of his life. Some historians believe that when the assassin bug bit into Darwin for a blood snack, it transmitted a dangerous disease.

▲ VAMPIRE BEETLE
The person on which this assassin bug has landed will not feel a thing, as the bug has injected a pain killer. These bugs are found world wide, especially in the tropics. Most of them hunt minibeasts and suck their juices dry.

EATEN ALIVE ►
Although most shield bugs are plant-eaters, this one is not. Some species start their lives as herbivores and move on to a mixed diet later. This one has caught a caterpillar, and uses its curving mouthparts to suck its prey dry. The bugs use their front legs to hold their victims steady while they feast on them.

shield bug

Did you know? Bedbugs check the smell and temperature of hosts before feeding on them.

◄ NO ESCAPE
When attacked, snails withdraw into their shells and seal them with slime, but this is no defence against a snail-hunting beetle, which squirts liquid into the shell to dissolve the slime and kill the snail. The snail-hunters usually have narrow heads that they can push right inside the shells.

tunnel left by leaf-mining caterpillar

Hungry Caterpillars

Caterpillars are streamlined eating machines. They must store enough energy to turn into adult moths or butterflies. Their bodies are like expandable sacks, fitted with strong mandibles (jaws) that are edged with teeth or blunt grinding plates. Caterpillars munch through several times their own body weight of food in a single day, and grow incredibly fast.

A caterpillar's first meal is usually the eggshell from which it has hatched. It then moves on to the next food source. Some species eat unhatched eggs or even other caterpillars. Most feed on the leaves and stems of a particular food plant—which is usually the one on which they hatched. The caterpillar stage lasts for at least two weeks, and sometimes much longer.

▲ LEAF MINING

Many tiny caterpillars eat their way through the inside of a leaf instead of crawling across the surface. This activity is known as leaf mining. Often, their progress is revealed by a pale tunnel beneath the leaf surface.

swallowtail butterfly caterpillar
(Papilio machaon)

sensitive palps are located near the mouth

legs are used to grip leaves while eating

▲ FEEDING HABITS

Caterpillars eat different food plants from those visited by adult insects. Swallowtail butterfly caterpillars feed on fennel, carrots and parsley. The adult butterflies drink the nectar of many different flowers.

IDENTIFYING FOOD ▶

The head end of a privet hawk moth caterpillar is shown in close-up here. A caterpillar probably identifies food using sensitive organs called palps, which are just in front of the mouth.

◄ FAST EATERS

Cabbages are the main food of the caterpillars of the large white butterfly. These insects can strip a field of leaves in a few nights. Many farmers and gardeners kill caterpillars with pesticides. The caterpillar population may also be kept down by parasitic wasps that attack the caterpillars.

▲ PICKY EATER

Many caterpillars feed on trees. Some, such as the gypsy moth caterpillars, feed on almost any tree, but others are more fussy. This cecropia moth caterpillar feeds only on willow trees.

Alice in Wonderland

In Lewis Carroll's story Alice in Wonderland, *a pipe-smoking caterpillar discusses with Alice what it is like to change size. Carroll was probably thinking of how fast caterpillars grow as a result of their non-stop eating.*

▲ PROCESSIONARY CATERPILLARS

The caterpillars of processionary moths rest together in silken nests, and travel to their feeding areas in long lines. These insects are poisonous and do not hide from predators.

Butterfly Food

postman butterfly
(*Heliconius*)

Many flowers produce a sugary fluid called nectar. This attracts insects in search of a meal, including butterflies and bees. Butterflies and moths do not have jaws and teeth, as they did in the caterpillar stage of their development. Instead, they suck up fluids through long, tubular proboscises, which act like drinking straws. Most butterflies survive exclusively on nectar. They spend most of their brief lives flitting from flower to flower in search of this juice. Some woodland species extract sweet liquids from other sources, such as rotting fruit and sap oozing from wounds in trees. A few species even suck on dung. Butterflies rarely live for more than a few days, as none of their foods are very nutritious.

▲ POISONOUS PLANTS

The larvae of *Heliconius* butterflies feed on passion flowers in the rain forests of South America. They absorb the plant's poison. It does not hurt them, but makes them unpalatable to birds. The adult butterflies also feed on the plant. They can detoxify the poison.

▲ FRUIT EATERS

The first generation of comma butterflies appears each year in early summer. These insects feed on the delicate white blossoms of blackberries, because the fruit has not ripened at this time. The second generation appears in autumn, and feeds on the ripe blackberry fruits.

red admiral butterfly
(*Vanessa atalanta*)

▼ CIDER DRINKING

In autumn, butterflies such as the red admiral and the Camberwell beauty often feed on rotting fruit. Sometimes the juice has fermented to alcohol, and the red admiral may be seen reeling around as if drunk.

Did you know? The purple emperor butterfly often survives by sucking juices from the rotting bodies of dead animals.

◄ DRINKING STRAW

Many flowers have nectaries inside the blooms to draw insects on to their pollen sacs. The insects carry pollen onto other flowers as they feed and pollinate them. Some butterflies have very long proboscises to reach deep stores of nectar.

▲ HOVERING HAWK MOTHS

The day-flying hummingbird hawk moth gets its name from its habit of hovering in front of flowers like a hummingbird. It sips nectar from this mid-flight position, rather than landing on the flower. Hawk moths have the longest proboscises of all butterflies and moths. The proboscis of the Darwin's hawk moth is 12–14 inches long, which is about three times the length of its body.

► WOODLAND VARIETY

Many woodland butterflies extract juices from a variety of sources. The speckled wood butterfly sometimes sips nectar from bluebells. However, it feeds mainly on honeydew, the sugary secretion of tiny insects called aphids. The leaves of plants are often coated with honeydew.

▲ NIGHT FEEDER

Noctuid moths often sip nectar from ragworts in meadows by moonlight. In temperate countries, these moths mostly feed on warm summer nights. They get their name from the Latin word *noctuis*, which means night.

speckled wood butterfly
(Pararge aegeria)

79

Spider Traps

Many spiders catch their prey on a sticky web, but this is only one of many quite different ways of catching or trapping food. Some spiders lurk inside hidden tubes of silk or underground burrows and wait patiently. Silk threads around the entrance trip up passing insects and other small creatures. Inside the burrow, the spider feels the tug on its trip lines, giving it time to rush out and pounce on the prey before it can escape. Lie-in-wait spiders include trapdoor spiders, which have special spines on their fangs to rake away the soil as they dig their burrows.

▲ SILK DOORS

The lid of a trapdoor spider's burrow is made of silk and soil. The door fits tightly into the burrow opening and may be camouflaged with twigs and leaves. In areas liable to flooding, walls or turrets are built around the entrance to keep out the water.

a purse-web spider waits for an insect to land on its tube-like web

an insect is speared by the spider's sharp jaws

▲ A SILKEN TUBE

This purse-web spider has emerged from its burrow. It usually lies in wait for prey inside its tubular purse of densely woven silk. The tube is about 18 inches long and about the thickness of a finger. Part of it sticks out of the ground or from a tree trunk, and is well-camouflaged with debris.

▲ INSIDE A PURSE-WEB

The spider waits inside its silken purse for an insect to walk over the tube. It spears the insect through the tube with its sharp jaws and drags the prey inside.

▲ FUNNEL-WEB SPIDERS

The Sydney funnel-web is one of the deadliest spiders in the world. It lives in an underground burrow lined with silk. Leading from the mouth of the burrow is a funnel that can be up to 3 feet across. Trip wires are also strung from the funnel, so that when an insect hits one, the spider is alerted. The spider can dig its own burrow with its fangs, but prefers to use existing holes and cracks. Funnel-web spiders eat beetles, snails and other small animals.

▲ TRIP WIRES

The giant trapdoor spider may place silken trip lines around the entrance to its burrow to detect the movements of a passing meal. If it does not have trip lines, the spider relies on feeling the vibrations of prey through the ground. If it senses a meal is nearby, it rushes from the burrow to grab the prey in its jaws.

Did you know? Trapdoor spiders may live up to 20 years in their burrows.

a spider looks out for passing prey

silk door

a centipede enters the spider's burrow

open sock

the false bottom of the closed sock hides the spider

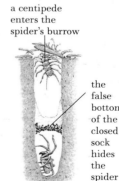

▲ ODD SPIDER OUT

A tiger wolf spider has dug out soil with its fangs and lined the walls of its burrow with silk. Most wolf spiders do not burrow. Instead, they chase their food, using their sharp vision and fangs to capture live insect prey.

▲ ALL KINDS OF TRAPS

Trapdoor spider burrows range from simple tubes to elaborate lairs with hidden doors and escape tunnels. The burrow of *Anidiops villosus* has a collapsible sock. The spider pulls it down to form a false bottom, hiding it from predators.

The Hunt of the

The salticid jumping spiders are a huge spider family of about 5,000 species. They are found all over the world, and most are squat, hairy and dull in color, although some tropical species have splashes of brilliant, iridescent color. All jumping spiders, however, have big, bulging eyes—all the better to hunt with! (If a human looks at a jumping spider, it will turn its tiny head to peer back.) As a family, salticids have the sharpest eyesight of any spider. Most species are constantly darting along jerkily, on the lookout for prey. They see in color and form clear images of their victims, stalking as a cat stalks a mouse, crouching before the final pounce.

SIGN LANGUAGE
A male jumping spider's front legs are longer and thicker than a female's. He waves them about in courtship dances, like a sign language.

PREPARATION
Before it takes off, a jumping spider anchors itself firmly to a surface with a silk safety line. It pushes off with its four back legs and leaps on to the target. The Australian flying spider has wing-like flaps that enable it to glide through the air.

STURDY LEGS
This female heavy jumper is feeding on a leaf-hopper. A jumping spider's legs do not seem to be specially adapted for jumping. Their small size (less than ¾ inch long) and light weight probably help them to make amazing leaps.

Jumping Spider

THE BIG LEAP

A jumping spider's strong front legs are often raised before a jump. They stretch forward in the air, and grip fast on the prey when the spider lands. Hairy tufts on the feet help jumping spiders to grip surfaces that are smooth and vertical. They can even leap away from a vertical surface to seize a flying insect.

JUMPING CANNIBALS

This female two-striped jumping spider is feeding on another member of the salticid family. Some *Portia* jumping spiders vibrate the webs of orb-weaving spiders, imitating the movement of an insect struggling to escape. When the orb-weaver comes to investigate, the *Portia* spider pounces on it.

A Snake's Rare Meal

Snakes are all predators, but different species eat different foods and hunt in different ways. Some snakes eat a wide variety of prey, while others have a more specialized diet. Snakes have to make the most of each meal because they move fairly slowly and may not catch prey very often. A snake's body works at a slow rate, which means that it can go for months without eating.

▲ TREE HUNTERS
A rat snake, from North America, grasps a baby bluebird in its jaws and begins the process of digestion. Rat snakes often slither up trees in search of baby birds, eggs or squirrels.

rat snake
(Elaphe)

▼ TRICKY LURE
The Australasian death adder's colorful tail tip looks like a worm. The adder wriggles the "worm" to lure birds and small mammals.

▲ FISHY SNACKS
The tentacled snake of southern Asia lives on fish. It hides among plants in the water and ambushes passing prey.

◄ EGG-EATERS
The African egg-eater snake checks an egg with its tongue to make sure it is fresh. Then it swallows the egg whole. It uses the pointed ends of the bones in its backbone to crack the eggshell. It eats the egg and then coughs up the crushed shell.

SURPRISE ATTACK ►
Lunch for this gaboon viper is a mouse. The viper hides among dry leaves on the forest floors of West and Central Africa. Its coloring and markings camouflage it well. It waits for a small animal to pass, then grabs hold of it in a surprise attack. Many other snakes that hunt by day also ambush their prey.

Did you know? Sometimes a snake coughs up its prey alive!

smooth snake
(*Coronella austriaca*)

◄ SNAKE SNACK
This smooth snake is eating an asp viper. The viper fits neatly inside the body of the smooth snake. This makes it easier to swallow than animals that are a different shape.

1 Rat snakes feed on rats, mice, voles, lizards, birds and eggs. Many of them hunt at night. They are good climbers and can even go up tree trunks with smooth bark and no branches. The snakes find their prey by following a scent trail or waiting to ambush an animal.

A Rat Snake's Lunch

Rat snakes are members of the world's largest snake family. They have more flexible skulls than more primitive snakes, such as pythons and boas, and their lower jaw is split into two unconnected halves. These adaptations enable the snakes to open their mouths very wide and to swallow their prey whole. The rat snake's favorite food are rodents such as voles and rats.

2 When the rat snake is near enough to its prey, it strikes quickly. Its sharp teeth sink into the victim's body to stop it running or flying away. The snake then loops its coils around the victim as fast as possible, before the animal can bite or scratch to defend itself.

3 Each time the vole breathes out, the rat snake squeezes around the victim's rib cage to stop it breathing in again. Breathing becomes impossible, and the victim soon dies from suffocation.

4 Once the victim is dead, the rat snake loosens its coils and begins the process of swallowing. It unhinges its jaws and "walks" its mouth over its meal. The loose lower jaw stretches sideways to fit around the shape of the dead prey.

5 The rat snake swallows its meal head first. As the vole moves down the snake's throat, its legs fold back against the sides of its body. The way the fur lies makes it easier to swallow the vole The snake's skin stretches as the meal moves down its body.

6 As the vole moves farther down inside the snake's body, the skin stretches more. The ribs move apart at the front to make space for the vole's body. The snake pushes its windpipe to the front of its mouth, so that it can use it like a snorkel for breathing. It may take only one or two gulps for a snake to swallow a small animal whole.

Crocodile Snacks

A big crocodile can survive for up to two years between meals. It lives off fat stored in its tail and other parts of its body. Generally, though, crocodilians (crocodiles, alligators and caimans) eat a lot of fish, although their strong jaws may snap up anything that wanders too close. Young crocodilians eat small animals such as insects, snails and frogs, while adults feed on birds, turtles and mammals. Big Nile crocodiles tackle large animals such as zebras and wildebeest when they visit the rivers to drink. Crocodiles cannot chew and have to tear large prey apart before swallowing it. They eat small prey whole, bones and all. Crocodiles also scavenge on dead animals.

Most crocodilians hunt at night and save energy by sitting and waiting for their food to pass their way. They may stalk prey, lunging forward or leaping out of the water to capture it. In water, a crocodile may sweep its open jaws from side to side to catch its next meal.

▲ **SURPRISE ATTACK**
A Nile crocodile lunges from the water at an incredible speed to grab a wildebeest in its powerful jaws. It is difficult for the wildebeest to jump back as the river bank slopes steeply into the water. The crocodile will plunge back into the water, dragging its prey with it in order to drown it.

▼ **CHEEKY BIRDS**
Large crocodiles feed on wading birds such as this saddlebill stork. Birds, however, often seem to know when they are in no danger from a crocodile. Plovers have been seen standing on the gums of crocodiles and even pecking at the fearsome teeth for leftovers. A marabou stork was once seen stealing a fish right out of a crocodile's mouth.

► SMALLER PREY

This dwarf caiman, hiding in floating debris, has just snapped up a tasty bullfrog. Caimans and other small crocodilians eat lots of frogs and toads, and also catch fish. The slim, pointed teeth of the Indian gharial are ideal for grasping any slippery fish that is within range, but its jaws are not strong enough to tackle anything bigger.

crocodilians have varied diets and will eat any animal they can catch

◄ SWALLOWING PREY

A crocodile raises its head and grips a crab firmly at the back of its throat. After several jerky head movements the crab is correctly positioned to be eaten whole. High levels of acid in the crocodile's stomach help it break down the crab's hard shell so that every part is digested.

Did you know? A Nile crocodile has a stomach that is about the size of a basketball.

► FISHY FOOD

A Nile crocodile swallows a fish head first so that the fish's spines do not stick in its throat. Fish make up about 70 percent of the diet of most crocodilians, especially the narrow snouted species, such as the gharial of northern India and the African slender-snouted crocodile. The narrowness of the snout offers little water resistance in the sideways sweeping movement used to catch fish.

Ambush on

1 A Nile crocodile is nearly invisible as it lies almost submerged in wait for its prey. Only eyes, ears and nostrils are showing. The crocodile lurks in places where it knows prey will regularly visit the river. The dark olive of its skin is well camouflaged against the murky water. It may disappear completely beneath the water. Some crocodilians can hold their breath for more than an hour while they are submerged.

A crocodile quietly drifting near the shore looks just like a harmless, floating log. This is just a disguise as it waits for an unsuspecting animal to come down to the river to drink. The crocodile is in luck. A herd of zebras come to cross the river. The crocodile launches its attack with astonishing speed. Shooting forwards, it snaps shut its powerful jaws and sharp teeth like a vice around a zebra's leg or muzzle. The stunned zebra is pulled into deeper water to be drowned. Other crocodiles are attracted to the large kill. They gather round to bite into the carcass, rotating in the water to twist off large chunks of flesh. Grazing animals constantly risk death-by-crocodile to drink or cross water. There is little they can do to defend themselves from the attack of such a large predator.

2 The crocodile erupts from the water, taking the zebras by surprise. It lunges at its victim with a fast burst of energy. The crocodile must overcome its prey quickly as it cannot chase a zebra overland. It is also easily exhausted and takes a long time to recover from exercise of any kind.

the River Nile

3 The crocodile seizes, pulls and shakes the zebra in its powerful jaws. The victim's neck is sometimes broken in the attack and it dies quickly. More often the shocked animal is dragged into the water, struggling feebly against its attacker.

4 The crocodile drags the zebra into deeper water and holds it down to drown it. It may also spin round in a roll, until the prey stops breathing. The crocodile twists or rolls around over and over again, with the animal clamped in its jaws, until the prey is dead.

5 A freshly killed zebra attracts Nile crocodiles from all around. A large kill is too difficult for one crocodile to defend on its own. Several crocodiles take it in turns to share the feast and may help each other to tear the carcass apart. They fasten their jaws on to a part of the body and turn over and over in the water until a chunk of meat is twisted loose and can be swallowed whole.

A Swift Attack from Above

sparrow hawk
(Accipiter nisus)

Birds of prey hunt in different ways. A raptor, which is another name for any bird of prey, may sit on a perch and simply wait for a meal to appear on the ground or fly past. This technique is called "still-hunting." Other birds search for prey by flying low over open ground, or darting in and out of cover such as a clump of trees. Kestrels are among the raptors that hover in the air while looking for prey, and then swoop down suddenly on it. Peregrine falcons are noted for their spectacular dives, or stoops. With wings almost folded, they dive on their prey from a great height, accelerating up to perhaps 185 miles per hour. Their aim is to strike the prey at high speed to kill it instantly. Peregrines either snatch prey from the air, or pick it off the ground.

▲ SURPRISE, SURPRISE

The sparrow hawk uses surprise and speed to make a kill. It flies under cover until it spots a potential meal, then dashes out into the open to snatch its unsuspecting prey at speed.

◄ PLUCKY EAGLE

An American bald eagle plucks a cattle egret it has just killed. The bird makes a change from the eagle's usual diet of fish. Most birds of prey pluck the feathers from birds they have caught before eating, as they cannot digest them. Owls are the only raptors to swallow their prey whole.

bald eagle
(Haliaeetus leucocephalus)

buzzard
(*Buteo buteo*)

◀ RABBIT RELISH

A common buzzard stands guard over the rabbit it has just killed. Over grassland, the buzzard hunts on the wing, sometimes hovering like a kestrel. Where there are trees or rocks, it may perch on a high point until it sights prey. The buzzard then swoops in for the kill.

▲ IN HOT PURSUIT

An African harrier hawk chases doves along the river bank. Such chases more often than not end in failure. This hawk is about the same size as a typical harrier, but it has longer wings.

▼ IT'S A COVER-UP

A kestrel spreads its wings in an attempt to cover up the mouse it is preparing to eat on its feeding post. This behavior is known as mantling, and is common among birds of prey. They do it to hide their food from other hungry birds that may try to rob them.

▼ MAKING A MEAL OF IT

A kestrel tucks into its kill on its favorite feeding post. The bird holds the prey with its feet and tears the flesh into small pieces with its sharp bill. It swallows small bones, but often discards big ones. Later, as with most raptors, it regurgitates pellets containing fur and other indigestible parts of its prey.

kestrel
(*Falco tinnunculus*)

Raptor Food

Birds of prey hunt all kinds of animals. Many attack other birds, such as sparrows, starlings and pigeons, which are usually taken in the air. Some raptors hunt small mammals, such as rabbits, rats, mice and voles. Large species of eagle may tackle even larger mammals. The Philippine eagle, and the harpy eagle of South America, for example, pluck monkeys from the rainforest canopy. Both species are massive birds, with bodies 3 feet long. Serpent eagles and secretary birds feast on snakes and other reptiles. Small birds of prey often feed on insects and worms. Most species will also supplement their diet by scavenging on carrion (the meat of dead animals) whenever they find it.

▲ **INSECT INSIDE**

A lesser kestrel prepares to eat a grasshopper it has just caught on a rooftop in Spain. This kestrel lives mainly on insects. It catches grasshoppers and beetles on the ground, and all kinds of flying insects while on the wing. When there are plenty of insects, flocks of lesser kestrels feed together. Unlike the larger common kestrel, the lesser kestrel does not hover when hunting.

golden eagle
(Aquila chrysaetos)

◄ **GOLDEN HUNTER**

A golden eagle stands guard over the squirrel it has just caught. This eagle usually hunts at low levels. It flushes out prey—mainly rabbits, hares and grouse—which it catches and kills on the ground. Whenever they get the chance, golden eagles also eat carrion.

martial eagle
(Polemaetus bellicosus)

The Fabulous Roc
In the tales of The Arabian Nights, *Sinbad the Sailor encountered enormous birds called rocs. They looked like eagles, but were gigantic in size, and preyed on elephants and other large beasts. In this picture, the fearsome rocs are dropping huge boulders on Sinbad's ship in an attempt to finally destroy him.*

▲ REPTILIAN SNACK

A martial eagle stands over its lizard kill in the Kruger National Park, South Africa. This is Africa's biggest eagle, and it is capable of taking prey as big as a small antelope.

Did you know? 12 species of birds of prey eat only insects.

▼ SNAIL SPECIALIST

A snail kite eyes its next meal. This is the most specialized feeder among birds of prey, eating only freshwater snails. It breeds in the Everglades National Park, Florida.

▲ COBRA KILLER

A pale chanting goshawk has caught and killed a yellow cobra. The chanting goshawks earned their name because of their noisy calls in the breeding season. The African plains are the hunting grounds of both the pale and the dark chanting goshawks, which feed mainly on lizards and snakes but also eat small mammals.

snail kite
(Rostrhamus sociabilis)

95

The Barn Owl's

1 An owl waits for a rustle in the undergrowth. Suddenly it hears something. It swivels its head, and its sensitive ears pinpoint exactly where the sound is coming from. The owl then spots its prey—a mouse rummaging among the leaf litter on the ground.

2 Keeping its eyes glued on its potential meal, the owl launches into the air. It brings its body forward, pushes off the post with its feet and opens its wings. The mouse is just a few yards away. It is busy searching for grubs and insects, and does not hear the swift, silent swoop.

The barn owl is found on all continents except Antarctica. It is easily recognizable because of its white, heart-shaped facial disc. Its eyes are relatively small for an owl, but it can still see well at night. The barn owl tracks its prey as much by ear as by eye. Its hearing is particularly keen, because the feathers on its facial disc channel sounds into its ears with great precision. The owl featured here is "still-hunting"—the tactic of watching for prey from a favorite perch. However, barn owls also often hunt on the wing. They cruise slowly and silently back and forth over their feeding grounds until they hear or spy prey, then swoop down silently for the kill.

Silent Strike

3 The owl makes a beeline for its prey with powerful beats of its wings. Even though it is travelling quite fast, it still makes no sound. Dense, soft feathers cover its wings and legs and muffle the sound of air flowing over them. Its noiseless flight allows the owl to concentrate on the sounds that the mouse is making and so keep track of its prey.

5 Now only a few inches above the ground, the owl thrusts its feet forward, claws spread wide, and drops on the prey. At the same time, it spreads its wings and tail to slow down the approach. The hunter's aim is deadly. Its talons close round the mouse and crush it to death. Then the owl transfers the dead mouse to its beak and returns to its perch. The owl will swallow the mouse head first.

4 The mouse at last begins to sense that something is wrong. For an instant it is glued to the spot in fear. Then it starts to run for its life. However, the owl is more than a match for it. By making use of its rounded wings and broad tail, the bird can twist and turn easily in the air, following the scuttling mouse at every change of direction.

Eating on the Hoof

The world's most successful herbivores (plant-eaters) are animals with hoofs, such as horses, cattle, deer and sheep. They use speed, endurance and sure-footedness to escape predators, and have digestive systems that make the most of vegetable diets. To convert low-quality food such as grass into body-building energy, an animal's digestive system has to break down tough cellulose fiber. One group of animals, which includes cattle, deer and sheep, do this by ruminating—they eat then later regurgitate the food, and chew it again slowly to draw as much goodness out of it as possible. Horses have a less efficient digestive system and have to spend more time eating than other grazers.

▲ RIVER HORSE

Hippopotamuses graze for a few hours each night, delicately plucking grasses with their broad, horny lips. Although they are huge animals, they can manage on about 90 pounds of grass each night because they rest in the water all day.

► HIGH LIVING

In Africa's open woodland savanna, giraffes browse the tops of trees that are out of reach to other herbivores. Their prehensile (grasping) lips and long, flexible tongues can pick out the most digestible and tasty leaves. Giraffes eat in the cool parts of the day and chew the cud while resting in the hot midday.

▲ TINY PUDU

The pudu of South America is the world's smallest deer. It lives in beech forests, feeding on flowers, fruit, bark and other vegetation. Like other deer and cattle, it spends a lot of its time resting and chewing the cud.

▲ TRAVELING COMPANIONS

The wildebeest, or gnu, are grazers of the African plains. Every dry season, when their food supply is exhausted, these big antelopes move to fresh pastures with permanent water and shade. They travel in vast herds along well-worn routes, joined by zebra and other grazing animals.

▼ HIGH-SPEED GAZELLE

Thomson's gazelles use the same food-plants as other grazers of the African plains, but each animal eats a different part of the plant. Zebras tackle the tough woody bits, wildebeest eat the leaves, and gazelles nibble at the new growth beneath.

▼ FIGHTING HORNS

Male bighorn sheep, like other ruminants, make use of their horns when defending their territory or their females. Bighorn sheep have adapted to a wide range of habitats in North America, from desert to chilly alpine areas. They establish seasonal pathways to fresh grazing grounds when food runs out in the harsh winters. As they bound over rocky ground, their padded feet grip and absorb the shock of impact.

▲ VARIED DIET

Warthogs feed almost entirely on grasses. After the rains, they pluck the growing tips with their incisor teeth or their lips. At the end of the rains they eat grass seeds, and in the dry season they use the hard upper edge of their nose to dig up roots.

Horse Power

Cows and other ruminants have an extra chance to chew every bit of goodness from their vegetable diet. Horses, however, have to gain their nutrients by eating more, but are able to survive and thrive on grass, the most nutrient-poor diet of all.

The horse's digestive system processes large quantities of food in order to extract enough energy. They have an extra-long digestive system—of around 100 miles—to push as much food as they can through their bodies and convert it quickly to energy. Horses run on a virtually nonstop cycle of eating, digesting and producing waste. In the wild, they graze for about 16 hours a day, from early in the morning until around midnight. Horses can survive on poor vegetation as long as there is plenty of it. Cattle can manage with less food, as long as it is of a reasonable quality.

▲ **CHEWING STYLE**
A horse's slow, deliberate style of eating ensures that food is thoroughly ground down. Horses nibble vegetation with their front incisor teeth, then grind it down with their molars before swallowing. They chew slowly and wash the food down with plenty of saliva to aid digestion.

◄ **HARD TIMES**
Cold weather has made the ground hard, and snow covers the scant winter vegetation. These horses must paw at the ground to uncover the grass and dig up roots. They may even eat tree bark. Weak horses may not survive a hard winter.

STRESS IN THE STABLE ▶

When domestic horses are brought into stables they are fed well but often only three times a day. This is very different from a horse's natural feeding pattern, which is continuous and varied grazing. Bored stabled horses sometimes develop "vices," such as crib-chewing, tongue swallowing and rug-chewing. Although a domesticated horse may be given nutritious fodder, it is starved of its natural behavior.

◀ SURVIVAL IN DRY LAND

Grevy's zebras live in dry thornbush country on the African plains. If water is scarce, they migrate to the highlands. They can survive, however, on grasses, or even bushes, that are too tough for other herbivores to eat. They also dig waterholes—and defend them fiercely.

▲ ALTERNATIVE FOODS

A horse from the New Forest, England, uses its flexible lips to pick some gorse flowers. Horses often choose more interesting foods than grass when they are available. They push out unwanted bits with their tongue.

▲ WATERHOLE

Wild horses drink daily, although they can go without water for long periods of time. Most animals only drink fresh water. Wild asses and some species of zebra can tolerate brackish (stale, salty) water. This gives them a better chance of surviving droughts than fellow grazers, such as antelope.

101

Elephant Appetites

As herbivores, elephants only eat plants. Their diet is much more varied than that of horses, however, as it is made up of more than 100 different kinds of plants. Elephants eat leaves, flowers, fruit, seeds, roots, bark and even thorns, but still need huge quantities to gain enough nutrients to survive. They spend about 16 hours a day picking and eating their food. As with cattle and horses, millions of microscopic organisms live inside an elephant's gut, which help it to digest food. Even with the help of these organisms, half the food eaten by an elephant is not digested when it leaves the body.

▲ STRIPPING BARK
An elephant munches on tree bark, which provides it with essential minerals and fiber. The elephant pushes its tusks under the bark to pull it away from the tree trunk. Then it peels off a strip by pulling with its trunk.

◄ EATING THORNS
Elephants do not mind swallowing a mouthful of thorns—as long as there are some tasty leaves attached. Leaves and thorns are an important part of an elephant's diet as they stay green in the dry season long after the grasses have dried up. This is because trees and bushes have long roots to reach water deep underground.

▼ GRASSY DIET
Marshes are packed full of juicy grasses. About 30—60 percent of an elephant's diet is grass. On dry land, an elephant may beat grass against its leg to remove the soil before feeding.

BABY FOOD ▶

Young elephants often feed on the dung of adult elephants. They do this to pick up microscopic organisms that will live inside their gut and help them digest food. Youngsters learn what is good to eat by copying their mothers and other adults. They are also curious and like to try new types of food.

◀ DUNG FOOD

Elephant dung provides a feast for dung beetles and thousands of other insects. They lay their eggs in the dung, and the young feed on it when they hatch. Certain seeds only sprout in dung after having first passed through an elephant.

EATING IN CAPTIVITY ▶

Meals for captive elephants include grasses and molasses (a type of sugar). Zoo elephants eat hay, bread, nuts, fruit, leaves, bark and vegetables. They need huge amounts. In the wild, elephants eat 225–450 pounds of plants every day—that equates to about 1,000–2,000 carrots!

Food in Season

Although bears are classified as meat-eating animals (carnivores), most of them eat whatever is available at different times of the year. They have binges and put on fat in times of plenty, then fast when food is scarce. Brown (grizzly) bears are typical of most bears in that they eat an enormous variety of food, from grasses, herbs and berries to ants and other insects. They also catch salmon, rodents and birds, and on rare occasions hunt bigger game, such as caribou and seals. Only polar bears eat almost entirely meat—usually young seals. In summer, however, they supplement their diet with grasses and berries. All bears, even bamboo-loving pandas, scavenge on the carcasses of prey left by other animals. To track down their food, bears rely mainly on their keen sense of smell. Their snouts are well-developed in relation to their small ears and eyes.

▶ HUNTING DOWN A MEAL

This American black bear has caught a white-tailed deer fawn. Both black and brown bears are successful hunters. They are able to ambush large animals and kill them by using their considerable bulk, strong paws and jaws. The size of the bear determines the size of its prey. Large brown bears may prey on moose, caribou, bison, musk ox, seals and stranded whales. The smaller black bears take smaller prey, such as deer fawns, lemmings and hares. Roots, fruit, seeds and nuts, however, form up to 80 percent of the diet of both species.

Goldilocks
Bears are often featured in children's stories, such as Goldilocks and the three bears. They are regularly portrayed as friendly animals. However, bears are not always so friendly, they plot to ambush their prey and use their size to overcome them.

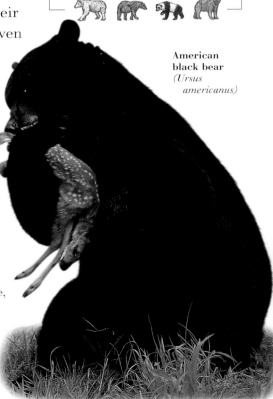

American black bear (*Ursus americanus*)

WALRUS CITY ▶

Polar bears arrive on the northern coast of Russia each summer to hunt walruses that have gone there to breed. Enormous adult walruses shrug off attacks, but the young walrus pups are more vulnerable.

▲ BEACHCOMBING

Brown bears visit rivers and estuaries, hoping for a fishy meal. They overturn stones to find crabs and crayfish underneath. Bears are also attracted to rubbish on beaches and campsites.

▲ FRUIT LOVERS

An American black bear snacks on the ripe berries of a mountain ash tree. It carefully uses its incisors (front teeth) to strip the berries from their woody stem.

▲ INSECT EATERS

Two sloth bear cubs from southern Asia learn to dig up termites. Sloth bears use their sickle-shaped claws to break open ant hills, bees' nests and termite mounds. They have developed an ingenious way of collecting their insect food. First they blow away any dust. Then they form a suction tube with mouth and tongue, through which they vacuum up their food.

Fishing Match

Grizzly and black bears sometimes overcome their reluctance to be with other bears when there is plenty of food available. This often happens on the rivers of the northwest coast of North America. Thousands of salmon come in from the sea and head upriver to spawn (lay their eggs). The bears fish alongside each other at sites such as rapids where the water is shallower and the salmon are easier to see. An uneasy truce exists between the bears, although isolated fights do occur. The salmon runs take place at different times of the year, but the most important are those in the months leading up to winter. The bears catch the oil-rich salmon to get the extra fat they need to see them through the long winter ahead.

▲ **STRIPPED TO THE BONE**
Having caught a fish, the bear holds it firmly in its forepaws. Then it strips the skin and flesh from the bones.

◀ **EASY MEAL**
Salmon sometimes jump right into a bear's mouth. The bear stands at the edge of a small waterfall. Here the salmon must leap clear of the water to continue their journey upriver. All the bear needs to do is open its mouth.

◄ FIGHT FOR SPACE

Sometimes the uncertain truce between bears breaks down and they fight for the best fishing sites in the river. Young bears playfight, but older ones fight for real. An open mouth, showing the long canine teeth, is a warning to an opponent. If the intruder fails to back down it is attacked. Fights are often soon over, because the bears are eager to return to their abundant source of fish.

▲ FISHING LESSON

Bear cubs watch closely as their mother catches a salmon. The cubs learn by example and will eventually try it themselves. It will be a long time before they are as skillful as their mother.

▲ A SLOUTHE OF BEERYS

A group of bears is called a sloth. Brown bears on a salmon river are "a sloth of grizzlies." The term "a slouthe of beerys" was used in the Middle Ages. It came from the word "sloth" (laziness) because people thought bears were slow and lazy.

Wild Cat Feasts

All big cats are carnivores (meat-eaters). In the wild, they hunt and kill their own food and also steal kills from other animals. Cheetahs, however, only eat animals they have killed themselves. They patrol their neighborhoods, stalking prey. Other cats, such as jaguars, hide in wait before ambushing their victims. Many cats, including leopards, employ both tactics. In either case, camouflage is vital. Many of their prey can outpace them over distances, so big cats have to creep close to their victims unnoticed before going in for the kill.

King Solomon
Solomon ruled Israel in the 900s BC and was reputed to be very wise. His throne was carved with lions because of his admiration for these big cats who killed only out of necessity. In law, if a missing person was said to have fallen into a lion's den, it meant that there was no proof of his or her death.

◀ **THE MAIN COURSE**
A lion can kill large, powerful animals such as buffalo. A big cat usually attacks from behind or from the side. The prey may be too big to kill right away. If so, the cat knocks it off balance, takes a grip and bites into its neck.

CHOOSING A MEAL ▶
A herd of grazing antelope and zebra keeps watch on a lioness crouched in the grass. The lioness lies as close to the ground as possible, waiting to pounce. When she has focused on a victim, she draws back her hind legs and springs forward.

▲ WARTHOG SPECIAL

Four cheetahs surround an injured warthog. The mother cheetah is teaching her three cubs hunting techniques. The cheetah on the right is trying a left paw side swipe, while another uses its claws. Cheetahs love to eat warthogs but also catch antelope and smaller animals such as hares.

▲ CAT AND MOUSE

A recently killed capybara (a large rodent) makes a tasty meal for a jaguar. Jaguars often catch prey such as fish and turtles in water. On land they hunt armadillos, deer, opossums, skunks, snakes, squirrels, tortoises and monkeys.

Did you know? Cheetahs will only chase prey if it runs. If it stops, so does the cheetah.

SLOW FOOD ▶

If a lion has not been able to hunt successfully for a while, it will eat small creatures such as this tortoise. Lions usually hunt big animals such as antelope, wildebeest, warthogs, buffalo, bush pigs and baboons. They work together in a group to hunt large prey.

Cats Go In for the Kill

Did you know? Lions try to flip porcupines onto their backs to avoid the sharp spines.

The way a wild cat kills its prey depends on the size of both predator and prey. If the prey is small with a bite-sized neck, it is killed with a bite through the spinal cord. Alternatively, a cat can crush the back of a small skull in its powerful jaws. Large prey is gripped by the throat so that it suffocates.

Cats stalk silently, their acute senses of sight, smell and hearing on the alert. Their large ears pick up the slightest sounds and can be turned to pinpoint the source of the sound.

▼ PAST ITS BEST
When big cats get old or injured it is very difficult for them to hunt. They eventually die from starvation. This lion from the Kalahari Desert in South Africa is old and thin. It has been weakened by hunger.

◄ FAIR GAME
A warthog is a delicious meal for a cheetah. Because the cheetah is quite a light cat, it must first knock over warthog-sized prey. It then bites the windpipe so that the victim cannot breathe.

▲ A DEADLY EMBRACE
A lioness immobilizes a struggling wildebeest by biting its windpipe and suffocating it. Lions are very strong. A lion weighing 330–550 pounds can kill a buffalo more than twice its weight. Lions live in groups called prides and the females do most of the hunting.

cheetah
(Acinonyx jubatus)

◄ **SECRET STASH**

A cheetah carrying off its prey, a young gazelle, to a safe place. Once it has killed, a cheetah will check the area to make sure it is secure before feeding. It drags the carcass to a covered spot in the bushes. Here it can eat its meal hidden from enemies. Cheetahs are often driven off and robbed of their kills by hyenas and jackals or even other big cats.

A SOLID MEAL ►

These cheetahs will devour as much of this antelope as they can. Big cats lie on the ground and hold their food with their forepaws when they eat. When they have satisfied their hunger, cheetahs cover up or hide the carcass with grass, leaves or whatever is available in order to save it for later.

► **LIONS' FEAST**

A pride of lions gathers around its kill. Lions often combine forces to kill large prey. One lion grabs the prey's throat, while the others attack from behind. The cats eat quickly before scavengers move in. Each has to wait its turn to eat. The dominant male usually eats first.

High-speed Cats

A cheetah is the world's fastest land animal. It can run at 70 miles per hour—the equivalent of a car being driven at high speed—but only over short distances. The cheetah's body is fine-tuned for short bursts of speed, with wide nostrils to breathe in as much oxygen as possible and specially adapted paws. Today, most cheetahs are found in east and southern Africa, with small populations in Iran and Pakistan. They live in many different kinds of habitats, from open grassland to thick bush, or even near-desert environments.

1 A pair of cheetahs creep up stealthily on a herd of antelope. Cheetahs hunt their prey by slinking slowly towards it, holding their heads low. They are not pouncing killers, like other big cats. Instead, they pull down their prey after a very fast chase. In order to waste as little energy as possible, cheetahs plan their attack first. They pick out their target before starting the chase.

2 The cheetah begins its chase as the herd of antelope starts to move. It can accelerate from walking pace to around 45 miles per hour in two seconds. Cheetahs have retractable claws (they can draw them in). However, unlike the claws of other cats, they have no protective sheaths. When drawn in, the exposed claws act like the spikes on the bottom of track shoes. This, combined with ridges on the paw pads, help cheetahs to grip when running.

3 At top speed a cheetah makes full use of its flexible spine and lean, supple physique. Its legs are very long and slender compared to its body. The cat can cover several yards in a single bound.

of the Plains

4 As the cheetah closes in on the herd, the antelope spring in all directions. The big cat changes direction at full speed. If it does not catch its prey within about 500 yards, it has to give up, as it can only keep up speed over short distances. Cheetahs usually hunt in the morning or late in the afternoon, when it is not too hot. Their life expectancy is short because their speed and hunting ability decline with age.

5 The cheetah may have to make several sharp turns as it closes in on its prey. Its long tail gives it excellent balance as it turns. The cheetah knocks its victim off balance with a swipe of a front paw. Most chases last no more than about 30 seconds.

6 Once the prey animal is down, the cheetah grabs the victim's throat. A sharp bite suffocates the antelope. Cheetahs are not strong enough to kill by biting through the spinal cord in the prey's neck like other big cats. They just hang on to the victim's throat until the animal is dead.

Hungry Canines

Wolves and other wild dogs are carnivores. They kill prey for fresh meat, but also eat carrion (dead animals). When no meat is available, they will eat fruit and berries, and also grass to aid digestion. As good long-distance runners, wild dogs can range over large territories in search of food. Packs of wolves target large herd animals such as moose, deer and caribou. They swim well and chase fish, frogs and crabs, but still spend much of their lives with empty bellies. When food is scarce, they sometimes rifle through rubbish near human settlements, or kill domestic animals such as sheep and cattle.

Most wild dogs have long, fanglike canine teeth to stab or pierce their prey. At the back of the mouth they have sharp-edged teeth for slicing through the flesh.

▲ NOT-SO-FUSSY FEEDERS

Raccoon dogs of eastern Asia eat all kinds of different foods, including rodents, fruit and acorns. Raccoon dogs also catch fish, frogs and water beetles and scavenge carrion and scraps from people's rubbish tips.

▼ CAUGHT BY COYOTES

Three coyotes tear at the carcass of a moose. These North American dogs usually hunt small prey such as mice. Sometimes they band together to go after larger creatures, or to gang up on other predators and steal their kills.

◄ FAST FOOD

A pack of dholes (an Asian species of wild dog) makes quick work of a deer carcass. Each dog eats fast to get its share—it may eat up to 9 pounds of meat in an hour. Dholes mainly eat mammals, but if meat is scarce they will also eat berries, lizards and insects.

▲ LONE HUNTER

A maned wolf is searching for food. Without a pack to help it hunt, this South American wolf looks for easy prey in open country, including armadillos and small rodents. It also eats birds, reptiles, insects, fruit and sugar cane.

▲ BEACH SQUABBLE

Two black-backed jackals squabble over the carcass of a seal pup. Jackals eat almost anything—fruit, frogs, reptiles and a wide range of mammals, from gazelles to mice. Jackals also scavenge kills from other hunters.

HIDDEN TREASURE ►

A wolf looks for a suitable spot in the snow to bury a freshly caught hare. After a pack has killed a large beast, or when a lone hunter has eaten its fill, it hides the remains of its food. Then, when food is scarce, the wolf can return to the hidden cache and retrieve its kill.

Did you know? All canids are quick feeders, but dholes in particular consume their food at a great rate.

gray wolf
(Canis lupus)

Wild Dog Hunt

The smaller species of wild dog, such as foxes and jackals, tend to hunt small prey, such as rodents, alone or in pairs. Some, including the solitary maned wolf, the bush dogs of the Americas and raccoon dogs, are mainly nocturnal (active at night). They rely on smell and hearing to find prey.

Dholes and African hunting dogs hunt in packs by day. They track prey by sight, smell and sound. Wolves hunt at any time of day or night. Hunting in packs means that larger prey can be tackled—ideally large enough to feed the whole pack. The size of a pack depends on the amount of food available in the area. Members of a pack work together like a sports team, with individuals providing particular strengths. Some may be good trackers, while others are fast or powerful. A hunt may last for several hours, but many are unsuccessful.

Little Red Riding Hood
In the story of Little Red Riding Hood, *a cunning wolf eats Red Riding Hood's grandmother. The wolf then steals the old woman's clothes to prey on the little girl. Fortunately a wood cutter rescues Red Riding Hood in the nick of time. After he kills the wolf, the grandmother emerges alive from inside its stomach.*

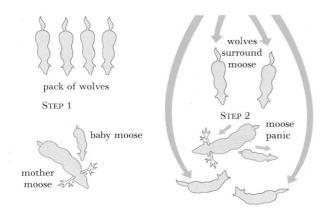

pack of wolves
STEP 1

baby moose

mother moose

wolves surround moose

STEP 2

moose panic

◄ **WOLF PACK IN ACTION**
Wolves use skill as well as strength to hunt large creatures such as moose. A calf is an easier target than an adult but will provide less meat. The wolves stalk their prey, then fan out and run ahead to surround the victim. Pack members dash forward to panic the animals and separate the mother from her baby. Once the young calf is alone, the wolves run it down and kill it by biting its neck.

DINGO KILL ▶

Two dingoes have just caught a kangaroo. In the Australian outback, dingoes hunt a wide range of creatures, from tiny grasshoppers and lizards to large prey such as wild pigs and kangaroos. Sheep, introduced by settlers in the 1800s, are a favorite target.

◀ **GROUP HUNTING**

A large pack of wolves has killed a white-tailed deer. This amount of meat will not satisfy the group for long. Where food is scarce, a pack has to range over a much larger territory to find enough food. A pack will always hunt the largest game it can find.

coyote
(*Canis latrans*)

CLEVER TACTICS ▶

A coyote plays with a mouse it has surprised in the snow. Coyotes often hunt mice. They leap high in the air to pounce on their victims. Coyotes have a more varied diet than wolves, feeding on fruit, grass, berries and insects, as well as mammals such as rabbits, deer and rodents. They take to the water to catch fish and frogs, and also steal sheep and chickens—which makes them unpopular with farmers.

Did you know To be in peak condition, a wolf needs to eat 9 pounds of meat a day.

▲ **TEAMWORK**

Working as a team, dholes hunt large prey such as sambar (a type of deer). Dholes whistle to keep in touch with one another as they surround their prey. Teamwork also helps the pack to defend the kill from scavengers such as vultures.

Hunting Dogs of

African hunting dogs eat more meat than any other wild dog. One in every three of their hunts ends in a kill, which is a very high success rate. They live on the savanna (grassy plains) of central and southern Africa, which is also home to vast herds of grazing animals such as wildebeest, gazelle and other antelopes. The pack wanders freely over a huge area, looking for herd animals to prey on. They rely on sight to find their quarry, so they hunt during daylight hours or on bright moonlit nights. They hunt mainly at dusk or dawn, when the air is coolest, and rest in the shade during the hottest time of day.

1 A pack of African hunting dogs begins to run down its quarry, a powerful wildebeest. On the open plains of the Serengeti in East Africa, there is little cover that would enable the dogs to sneak up on their prey. The hunt is often a straightforward chase. The hunt may be led by a junior dog at the start of the pursuit.

2 The dogs run along at an easy lope at first. They have tested out the wildebeest herd to find an easy target. They look for weak, injured, or young and inexperienced animals that will make suitable victims. This wildebeest is an older animal whose strength may be failing.

the African Plains

3 A hunting dog tries to seize the wildebeest's tail. Members of the pack with different strengths and skills take on particular roles during the hunt. The lead dogs are in excellent condition and strong. They dodge out of the way if the wildebeest turns to defend itself with its sharp hooves and horns. Fast runners spread out to surround the victim and cut off its escape.

4 As the wildebeest tires, two dogs grip its snout and tail, pinning it down. Hunting dogs can run at 30 miles per hour for quite a distance, but their prey is much quicker. While the lead dogs follow the fleeing animal's twists and turns, backmarkers take a more direct line to save their strength. The rear dogs take over the chase as the leaders tire.

5 More dogs arrive and the strongest move in for the kill. While some dogs hold their victim by the snout and flanks, others jump up to knock it off balance. The dogs attack their victim's sides and rump and soon the animal is bleeding freely. It begins to weaken through shock and loss of blood.

6 The wildebeest crashes to the ground and the dogs rip at its underparts to kill it There is little snapping and snarling as they eat, but the kill is fiercely defended if a scavenger such as a jackal comes close. Half-grown cubs feed first, then the carcass is ripped apart and bones, skin and all are eaten. Back at the den, meat is regurgitated to feed the cubs.

Forest Food for Apes

Apes live in the rainforests of Africa and Asia and feed on fruit and leaves. They also eat a small amount of animal food, such as insects. Chimpanzees have a more varied diet than other apes and occasionally eat red meat from birds and mammals, such as monkeys and young antelopes. Orangutans have also been seen eating young birds and squirrels.

Apes spend a lot of time traveling all over the forest to find their food. If they stayed in one place, they would quickly use up all the food. They remember the locations of the best fruit trees in their area, and know when they will bear fruit. Apes have to eat a lot because a diet that consists mainly of plant food is often low in nutrients. As they cannot digest the tough fibers (cellulose) in the stems and leaves, much of what they eat passes through their gut undigested.

▲ HUNGRY GIBBON

Gibbons, from Southeast Asia, are mainly frugivores (fruit eaters) but they also eat leaves and occasionally insects and eggs. They are so light and have such long arms that they can hang from thin branches and pick the ripest fruit growing right at the ends.

▶ BANANA BONANZA

Orangutans live in the forest canopies of Southeast Asia. Fruit forms about 65 percent of their diet. The apes spread the seeds over a wide area by passing them in their droppings far from the parent tree. This female has found some bananas, but the football-sized fruit of the durian tree is another orangutan favorite. It contains a sweet-tasting but foul-smelling flesh, which they adore.

▲ MASSIVE MEALS

Gorillas are mainly herbivores, munching their way through 45–65 pounds of greens (equal to 40 cabbages) every day. They smack their lips a lot and make other appreciative noises. Gorillas are careful eaters, often preparing their food by folding leaves into a roll, or peeling off inedible layers. They drop any unwanted stalks, in a neat pile.

▲ RAIDING PARTY

Chimpanzees live in communities in west and central Africa. They eat both meat and vegetable matter and may band together to form a raiding party to hunt small animals such as monkeys and bush pigs. A hunt may last up to two hours, involving high-speed chases and ambushes.

▼ CHIMP FEASTS

Chimpanzees spend about six hours a day feeding, mostly just after sunrise and just before sunset. They eat a lot of fruit, which makes up about 68 percent of their diet, but they also eat leaves and other plant matter, as well as meat and insects.

▲ FOOD ALL AROUND

The upland rainforests of central and eastern Africa are full of plant food for the mountain gorillas that live there. They eat leaves, roots and fruit, soft bark and fungi. The gorillas need to eat a lot of food, so meals last two to four hours at a time. They have big stomachs to store the food while it is being digested. Gorilla days are mainly spent walking and eating food, then resting between meals to digest it.

chimpanzee
(Pan troglodytes)

121

Whale Feeding

About 90 percent of whales have pointed teeth that are ideal for grasping slippery fish. The other ten percent, known as baleen whales, do not have any teeth. Brush-like plates of horny baleen hang from the upper jaw. A baleen whale takes a mouthful of seawater and sieves it out through the baleen plates. Food, such as fish, algae and krill is held back in the baleen, and then swallowed. Toothed whales catch single fish, while baleen whales eat a mass at one time.

▲ **CRUNCHY KRILL**
These tiny shrimplike creatures known as krill form the diet of many baleen whales. Measuring up to 3 inches long, they swim in vast shoals, often covering areas of several square miles. Most krill are found in Antarctic waters.

◄ **PLOWING**
A gray whale plows into the seabed, stirring up sand and ooze. It dislodges tiny crustaceans, called amphipods, and gulps them down. Grey whales feed mostly in summer in the Arctic before they migrate south.

southern right whale
(*Euhalaena australis*)

◄ **SKIM FEEDING**
With its mouth open, a southern right whale filters crustaceans, called copepods, out of the water with its baleen. The whale is huge, up to 80 tons, and it needs to eat up to two tons of the copepods daily. Usually, right whales feed alone, but if food is plentiful, several feed as they cruise side by side.

◄ **SUCCULENT SQUID**

Squid is the sperm whale's favorite food and is eaten by other toothed whales and dolphins as well. Squid are mollusks, in the same animal order as snails and octopuses. They have eight arms and two tentacles, and are called decapods (meaning ten feet). Squid sometimes swim together in dense shoals, of thousands.

◄ **TOOTHY SMILE**

A Ganges river dolphin has more than 100 teeth. The front ones are very long. Ganges river dolphins eat mainly fish, and also take shrimps and crabs. They usually feed at night and find their prey by echolocation.

Did you know? A blue whale eats nearly 2,250 pounds of krill in a single meal.

Ganges river dolphin
(Platanista gangetica)

SUCKING UP A MEAL

Belugas feed on squid, small fish and crustaceans. Unlike common dolphins, belugas do not have many teeth. They suck prey into their mouths and then crush it with their teeth. Beaked whales also suck in their prey—mainly deep-sea squid—as their teeth are not suitable for grasping hold of fish.

▲ **HUNT THE SQUID**

The sperm whale is the largest toothed whale, notable for its huge head and tiny lower jaw. It hunts the giant squid that live in waters around 6,500 feet deep. At that depth, in total darkness, it hunts its prey by echo-location.

A Killer Whale

Among the toothed whales, the killer whale, or orca, is the master predator. It bites and tears its prey to pieces with its fearsome teeth and may also batter them with its powerful tail. It is the only whale to take warm-blooded prey. It may even attack a large baleen whale many times its size. As well as hunting seals, penguins, dolphins and porpoises a killer whale will also hunt fish and squid. Fortunately, there is no record of a killer whale ever attacking human beings. Killer whales live in family groups called pods. They often go hunting together, which greatly improves the chance of success.

1 A killer whale hunts by itself if it comes upon a likely victim, such as a lone sea lion. This hungry whale has spotted a sea lion splashing in the surf at the water's edge. With powerful strokes of its tail, it surges towards its prey. The whale's tall dorsal fin shows that it is a fully grown male.

2 The sea lion seems totally unaware of what is happening but, in any case, it is nearly helpless in the shallow water. The belly of the killer whale is scraping the shore as it homes in for the kill.

on a Seal Hunt

3 Suddenly the killer's head bursts out of the water, and its jaws gape open. Vicious teeth, curving inward and backward, are exposed. It is ready to sink them into its sea lion prey. The killer whale has fewer teeth than most toothed whales, but they are large and very strong.

4 Now the killer snaps its jaws shut, clamping the sea lion in a vicelike grip. With its prey struggling helplessly, it slides back into deep water to eat its fill. Killer whales are in danger of stranding themselves on the beach when they lunge after prey. They usually manage to wriggle their way back into the sea with the help of the surf.

Sea Hunters

Most sharks are fearful carnivores and streamlined swimmers with an amazing sense of smell. Some make the most of their powerful, torpedo-shaped bodies to chase or pounce suddenly upon their prey. Others can be more leisurely, as they have special tracking and hunting adaptations. The lantern shark has organs on its skin that produce light and lure prey to certain death. The wide-spaced eyes of the hammerhead give it a wide field of vision to spot its favorite food, sting rays. The shortfin mako is one of the world's fastest sharks and can leap high above the water's surface. The white shark can leap, too, and has an awesome set of razor-sharp teeth to rip into large prey such as seals and dolphins.

▲ **FEEDING FRENZY**
Large quantities of food will excite grey reef sharks, sending them into a feeding frenzy. If divers hand out food, the sharks will circle with interest, until one darts forward for the first bite. Other sharks quickly follow, grabbing at the food until they seem out of control.

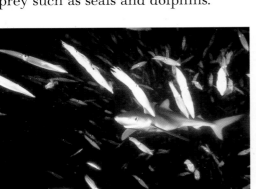

▲ **FOREVER EATING**
A large shoal of mating squid provides a great feast for blue sharks. The sharks feed until full, then empty their stomachs to start again!

▲ **FISH BALL**
A group of sharks can herd shoals of fish into a tight ball. The sharks will then pick off fish from the outside of the ball, one by one.

▶ NOT POWERFUL ENOUGH

The black-tipped shark is generally a powerful swimmer, but this one was caught by a larger relative, the bull shark. Black-tipped sharks hunt in the shallow waters of tropical seas, using their amazing sense of smell. Small fish hide out of reach in rocky crevices to escape.

Did you know? The great white shark sometimes eats crabs and lobsters.

◀ OCEAN DUSTBIN

Most sharks will eat anything that swims into their territory, and many are scavengers. Tiger sharks, though, are notorious for the variety of their diet. They have been known to eat coal, rubber tires, clothes—and humans—and they move into coastal waters at night to feed. They are found all over the world and grow to a length of 18 feet.

▼ BITESIZE CHUNKS

The cookie-cutter shark feeds by cutting chunks out of whales and dolphins, such as this spinner dolphin. The shark uses its mouth like a clamp, attaching itself to its victim. It then bites with its razor-sharp teeth and swivels to twist off a circle of flesh.

spinner dolphin
(*Stenella longirostris*)

▲ OPPORTUNISTS

Sharks will often follow fishing boats, looking for a free meal. This silvertip shark is eating pieces of tuna fish that have been thrown overboard.

127

How Animals Communicate

The way that animals interact with each other can be a vital factor in their survival. Some animals live together in groups while others live alone. This section looks at some of the most social animals on earth, explaining how their communities work. It also looks at some of the animals that are usually solitary and explains why they find it better to live alone.

Communicating in the Wild

Animals "talk" to each other in many different ways. Most forms of communication are with other individuals of the same kind, but many animals also send signals to other species. These signals are usually concerned with defence. Rattlesnakes, for example, rattle their tails to warn predators or any other large animals that they might get hurt if they get any closer. Many poisonous or bad-tasting insects, including the Monarch butterfly, are brightly colored. Predators might try them once or twice, but they soon learn that the brightly colored insects taste bad and should be left alone. Some animals even give out signals to trick their prey. The snapping turtle, for example, attracts fishes to its mouth by waggling its wormlike tongue.

The bright colors of the Monarch butterfly warn predators to stay away.

Communicating with the neighbors

Nearly every species uses some kind of signal to attract mates. Male crickets and grasshoppers attract females with their chirpy "songs." Many birds also use songs, although others, including most birds of prey, rely more on spectacular aerial displays. Some male spiders also perform elaborate dances in front of the females. Scents—given out by one or both sexes—play a major role in the courtship and mating of most animals. Mating signals are the only forms of communication used by some solitary animals (those animals that live alone) but most species have a much more complex range of signals.

The most complex "language" is found among the social animals—those that live in groups and cooperate with each other. They use sounds, visual signals, and scents to pass information to each other. Touching each other is also an important method of giving and receiving information. One of the most amazing forms of communication is the dance language of honeybees. A worker bee finding a good source of nectar returns to the hive and dances on the honeycombs. Other workers join in the dance, and the direction and speed of the action tells them the direction and distance of the nectar. They then fly off to collect more of this important food.

Wolves are sociable animals and use touch to bond with each other. They rub bodies, lick each other, and nuzzle each other's fur when they meet.

Communicating by sound

The songs of many male birds attract mates, but they also help to defend a territory by telling other males to keep away. Gibbons and howler monkeys also use sounds to stake out their territories. Chimpanzees are very noisy and excitable animals and they use more than 30 different grunts, screams and hoots to talk to each other. Elephants also make a wide variety of calls, including strange tummy rumbles, some of which can be heard several miles away. Dolphins talk to each other by way of an amazing variety of clicks and whistles as they swim through the water.

Dolphins communicate by making high-pitched sound waves by vibrating the air in the passages in their nose. The waves are focused into a beam through the bulge on their head. This sound is then transmitted into the water.

Body language

Many social animals convey their moods and messages by the way they stand or move. Horses and elephants signal to other herd members by moving their ears. The members of a wolf pack all get on well together because each animal knows its place. A low-ranking wolf lowers its head and puts its tail between its legs when it meets a higher ranking individual, as if saying "You're the boss and I won't cause any trouble." A male gorilla makes sure that the other clan members know he is in charge by standing and thumping his chest. Chimpanzees make faces to indicate their various moods, such as fear, anger, or playfulness. An angry chimp, for example, clenches its lips shut.

Gorillas communicate with a variety of sounds, facial expressions and gestures. They stand on their back legs and beat their chests rapidly with their hands. Gorillas very rarely fight with each other, and this is a display to scare away rivals.

Getting close

Chimpanzees, horses, wolves, lions and many other animals spend a lot of time nuzzling and licking each other. This is known as grooming and it helps to keep all the members of a group on good terms. Ants and other social insects also touch and feed each other. This helps to spread the pheromones (bodily scents) that keep the colonies running smoothly.

When members of a zebra herd meet up, they welcome each other with a series of greeting rituals that include touching and sniffing. Good friends sometimes lay their heads on each other's back.

131

Bee and Wasp Colonies

Social bee and wasp colonies work like miniature, smooth-running cities. Like good citizens, all the insects in the colony instinctively know their roles and carry out their tasks.

In a honeybee colony, the workers perform different tasks according to their age. The youngest workers stay in the nest and spend their first weeks cleaning out the brood cells. Later they feed the young. As the wax glands in their abdomen develop, they help build new cells. They also keep the nest at the right temperature. After about three weeks, the worker honeybees go outside to fetch nectar and pollen to store or to feed their sisters. The oldest, most-experienced workers act as guards and scouts. Many wasp colonies work in a similar way, with workers doing different jobs according to their age.

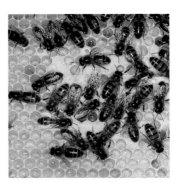

▲ **ADJUSTING THE HEAT**
Honeybees are very sensitive to tiny changes in temperature. The worker bees adjust the temperature around the brood cells to keep the air at a constant 90°F. In cold weather, they cluster together to keep the brood cells warm. In hot weather, they spread out to create cooling air channels.

◄ **NEST REPAIRS**
Worker honeybees use a sticky tree resin to repair cracks in their nest. This gummy material is also known as propolis or "bee glue". The bees carry it back to the nest in the pollen baskets on their hind legs. If there is no resin around, the bees may use tar from roads instead.

▲ **BUILDING NEW CELLS**
Honeybee cells are made by workers using wax from their abdomens. The bees use their antennae to check the dimensions of the cells as they must be the right size to fit the young.

◀ THREAT DISPLAY

Paper wasp workers from Equador in South America swarm over the outside of their nest to frighten off intruders. Like all wasp workers, one of their main roles is to defend the nest. If this display fails, the wasps will attack and sting their enemy. However, most animals will retreat as quickly as they can.

▲ PRECIOUS CARGO

A worker honeybee unloads her cargo of nectar. The bees use the nectar to make honey, which is a high-energy food. The honeybee workers eat the honey, which allows them to survive long, cold winters in temperate regions, when other worker bees and wasps die.

TENDING THE YOUNG ▶

A honeybee tends the larvae (young bees) in the nest cells. Honeybees feed their young on nectar and pollen from flowers. Wasp workers feed their larvae on balls of chewed-up insects. The young sister is allowed to feed for about ten seconds, then the worker remoulds the food ball and offers it to another larva. The adult may suck juices from the insect meat before offering it to the young.

◀ LITTLE BUMBLEBEE NESTS

Social bumblebees, shown here live in much smaller colonies than honeybees. European bumblebee nests usually hold between 20–150 insects, whereas a thriving honeybee colony may hold 60–80,000 insects. The queen bumblebee helps her workers with the day-to-day running of the nest as well as laying eggs.

133

Ant and Termite Societies

Like bee and wasp societies, ant colonies are all-female for much of the year. Males appear only in the breeding season to mate with the young queens. Ant colonies are tended by hundreds or thousands of sterile female workers. The worker ants also fight off enemies when danger threatens, repair and expand the nest, and adjust conditions there. Some ants use the workers from other species as 'slaves' to carry out these chores.

In most types of ants, the large queen is still nimble and active. However, the termite queen develops a huge body and becomes immobile. She relies on her workers to feed and care for her, while she produces masses of eggs.

▲ ON GUARD
These ants are guarding the cocoons of queens and workers, who will soon emerge. One of the workers' main tasks is to defend the colony. If you disturb an ants' nest, the workers will rush out with the cocoons of young ants and carry them to a new, safe site.

▼ RIVER OF ANTS
Safari ants march through the forest in long lines called columns. The workers, carrying the cocoons of young ants, travel in the middle of the column, where it is safer. They are flanked by a line of soldiers on each side. Resembling a river of tiny bodies, the column may stretch more than 300 feet.

▲ ANT RAIDERS
Slavemaker ants survive by raiding. Here an ant is carrying off a worker from another species. Some slavemakers, such as red Amazon ants, have sharp, pointed jaws that are good for fighting, but no use for other tasks. They rely on ant slaves to gather food and run the nest.

◄ TERMITE SKYSCRAPER

These African termite workers are building a new ventilation chimney for their nest. African termites build the tallest towers of any species, up to 25 feet high. If humans were to build a structure of the same height relative to our body size, we would have to build skyscrapers that were more than 6 miles high. The tallest skyscraper today is less than 1,650 feet tall.

FAMILY LIFE ►

A queen termite is flanked by the king (the large insect below her), workers and young termites. The king and queen live much longer than the workers — for 15 years or even more in some species. The queen may lay 30,000 eggs in a day — that is one every few seconds. The king stays at her side in the royal chamber and fertilizes all the eggs.

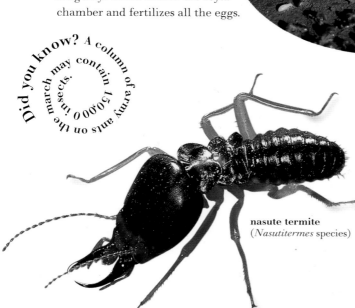

Did you know? A column of army ants on the march may contain 150,000 insects.

◄ BLIND GUARD

A soldier termite displays its huge head, which is packed with muscles to move the curved jaws at the front. Being blind, the guard detects danger mainly through scent, taste and touch. Like termite workers, soldiers may be either male or female, but they do not breed. The arch-enemies of these plant-eating insects are meat-eating ants, which hunt them for food.

nasute termite
(*Nasutitermes* species)

How Social Insects

Communication is the key to the smooth running of social insect colonies. Colony members interact using smell, taste, touch and sound. Social insects that can see also communicate through sight. Powerful scents called pheromones are the most important means of passing on information. These strong smells, given off by special glands, are used to send a wide range of messages that influence nestmates' behavior. Workers release an alarm pheromone to rally their comrades to defend the colony. Ground-dwelling ants and termites smear a scent on the ground to mark the trail to food. Queens give off pheromones that tell the workers she is alive and well.

THE QUEEN'S SCENT
Honeybee workers lick and stroke their queen to pick up her pheromones. If the queen is removed from the nest, her supply of pheromones stops. The workers rear new queens who will produce the vital scents.

TERMITE PHEROMONES
A queen termite spends her life surrounded by workers who are attracted by her pheromones. The scents she releases cause her workers to fetch food, tend the young and enlarge or clean the nest.

FRIEND OR FOE?
Two black ants meet outside the nest and touch antennae to identify one another. They are checking for the particular scent given off by all colony members. Ants with the correct scent are greeted as nestmates. 'Foreign' ants will probably be attacked.

Communicate

THIS WAY, PLEASE

A honeybee worker exposes a scent gland in her abdomen to release a special scent that rallies her fellow workers. The scent from this gland, called the Nasonov gland, is used to mark sources of water. It is also used like a homing beacon to guide other bees during swarming, when the insects fly in search of a new nest.

ALARM CALL

These honeybees have come to the hive entrance to confront an enemy. When alarmed, honeybees acting as guards give off an alarm pheromone that smells like bananas. The scent tells the other bees to come to the aid of the guards against an enemy. In dangerous "killer bee" species, the alarm pheromone prompts all hive members to attack, not just those guarding the nest.

SCENT TRAIL

This wood ant worker has captured a worm. The ant is probably strong enough to drag this small, helpless victim back to the nest herself. A worker that comes across larger prey returns to the nest to fetch her comrades, rubbing her abdomen along the ground to leave a scent trail as she does so. Her fellow workers simply follow the smelly trail to find the food. Ants can convey as many as 50 different messages by releasing pheromones and through other body language.

The Butterfly's Mating Quest

common blue butterfly
(Polyommatus icarus)

Butterflies are usually solitary insects. Although hundreds of thousands of them sometimes migrate together, this is not true social behavior because they do not cooperate with each other. The butterflies don't work together as a group, or communicate. However, all butterflies do need to communicate with each other when looking for a mate.

Most males court females with elaborate flights and dances. Males and females are drawn to each other by the shape of each other's wings and by their colorful patterns. Both sexes also emit pheromones to encourage their mate. Courting butterflies circle each other, performing complicated dances.

▲ **COURTING BLUES**
When courting a female, a male butterfly often flutters its wings flamboyantly. It looks as if it is showing off, but it is really wafting around its pheromones (the scents from special scales on its forewings). Only if the female picks up these pheromones with her antennae will she be willing to mate.

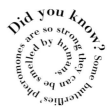

Did you know? Some butterflies' pheromones are so strong they can be smelled by humans.

◄ **THE HAPPY COUPLE**
This pair of butterflies is about to mate. When she is ready, the female (right) flies away and lands with her wings half open. The male flutters down on top of her and begins to caress her abdomen with his rear end. The male then turns around to face the opposite way as they couple. The pair may remain joined for hours.

Madame Butterfly

One of the most famous operas is Puccini's "Madame Butterfly", written in 1904. The opera is set in the 1800s in Osaka, Japan. It tells the story of an American officer, James Pinkerton, who falls in love with a beautiful young Japanese girl. His nickname for her is Butterfly. They have a child, but Pinkerton abandons Butterfly for his wife in America. The opera ends as Butterfly dies broken-hearted.

▼ SCENT POWER

A butterfly's scent plays a major role in attracting a mate. The scents come from glands on the abdomen of a female. On a male, the scents come from special wing scales called androconia. A male often rubs his wings over the female's antennae.

androconia scales
release scent

▼ COLORS ATTRACT

Many male butterflies use bright colors to attract mates. This male orange-tip has a distinctive colored tip to its wings. Females often lack bright colors so are less obvious.

male orange-tip butterfly
(Anthocharis cardamines)

▼ SINGLE MATE

Male butterflies mate several times in their lifetime. However a female butterfly usually mates just once and then concentrates on egg-laying. Once they have mated, many females release a special pheromone that deters other males.

female orange-tip butterfly
(Anthocharis cardamines)

▲ FLYING TOGETHER

Butterflies usually stay on the ground or on a plant while coupling. But, if they sense danger, they can fly off linked together, with one (the carrier) pulling the other backwards.

Spider

Although some spiders look after their young, most species only need to communicate with each other when they are ready to mate. Female spiders attract males by giving off pheromones. Each species has a different pheromone, to help the males find the right mate. Once he has found a female, the male has to give out the right signals so that the female realizes he is not a meal. These include special dances, drumming, buzzing, or plucking the female's web in a particular way. Some males distract the females with a gift of food.

NOISY COURTSHIP
The male buzzing spider beats his abdomen against a leaf to attract a mate. The sound is loud enough for people to hear. He often buzzes on the roof of the female's oak-leaf nest. Other male hunting spiders make courtship sounds by rubbing one part of their bodies against another.

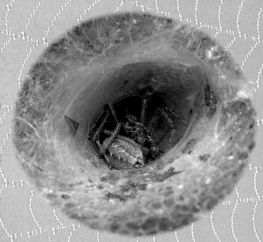

MATING SUCCESS
The male grass funnel-weaver is almost as large as the female and can be quite aggressive. He taps his palps (leg-like feelers) on her funnel web to announce his arrival. If the female is ready to mate, she draws in her legs and collapses as if she is paralysed.

the male (left) presents a gift to the female

BEARING GIFTS
A male nursery-web spider presents an insect gift to the female. He has neatly gift-wrapped his present in a dense covering of very shiny white silk. Once the female has accepted his gift and is feeding, the male can mate with her in safety.

140

Courtship

DISTANT DANCE
Spiders that can see well at a distance often dance together before mating. This wolf spider waves his palps like semaphore flags to a female in the distance. Male spiders also strike special poses and use their long, strong front legs to make signaling more effective.

A RISKY BUSINESS
Male garden spiders often have great difficulty courting a female. They are usually much smaller and lighter than the female and have to persuade her to move onto a special mating thread. The male joins the mating thread to the edge of the female's web. He then tweaks the silk strands of her web to lure the female towards him.

DANGEROUS LIAISONS
This male green orb-weaver has lost four of his legs in the process of courting a female. When the female attacked him, he swung down a silken dragline (escape line). He will climb back up again when it is safe.

JUMPING SPIDERS
This pair of jumping spiders are ready to mate. Male jumping spiders impress females by twirling and waltzing, waving their legs, palps and abdomens. Females often attract more than one male and the males have to compete to mate with her. The female reaches out and touches the male when she is ready to mate.

141

Crocodile Talk

Most reptiles spend very little time with each other, but crocodiles, alligators and other crocodilians have a remarkably sociable life. Groups gather together for basking in the sun, sharing food, courting and nesting.

Crocodilians use sounds, body language, smells and touch to communicate. Adults are particularly sensitive to hatchling and juvenile distress calls and respond with threats or actual attacks. Sounds are made with the vocal cords and with other parts of the body, such as slapping the head against the surface of the water. Crocodilians also use visual communication. Body postures and special movements show which individuals are strong and dominant. Weaker animals signal to show that they recognize a dominant individual and in this way avoid fighting and injury.

▲ **HEAD BANGER**
A crocodile lifts its head out of the water, jaws open. The jaws slam shut just before they smack the surface of the water. This is called the head slap and makes a loud pop followed by a splash. Head slapping may be a sign of dominance and is often used during the breeding season.

The Fox and the Crocodile
In this Aesop's fable, the fox and the crocodile met one day. The crocodile boasted at length about its cunning as a hunter. Then the fox said, "That's all very impressive, but tell me, what am I wearing on my feet?" The crocodile looked down and there, on the fox's feet, was a pair of shoes made from crocodile skin.

▲ **GHARIAL MESSAGES**
The gharial does not head slap, but claps its jaws under water during the breeding season. Sound travels faster through water than air, so sound signals are very useful for aquatic life.

THE LOW SOUND ▶

Some crocodilians make sounds by rapidly squeezing their torso muscles just beneath the surface of the water. The water bubbles up and bounces off the back. The sounds produced are at such a low level we can hardly hear them. At close range, they sound like distant thunder. Very low sounds, called infrasounds, travel quickly over long distances through the water. They may be part of courtship. Sometimes these sounds are produced before bellowing, roaring or head slaps.

Did you know? The bellow of an alligator can be heard at least 50 feet away.

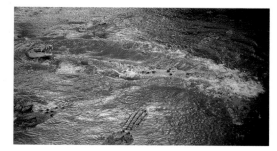

◀ I AM THE GREATEST

Dominant animals are usually bigger and more aggressive than submissive ones. They show off their importance by swimming boldly at the surface or thrashing their tails from side to side on land. When threatened, weaker individuals usually only lift their heads out of the water and expose their vulnerable throats. This shows that they submit and do not want to fight.

GETTING TOGETHER ▶

Caimans gather together at the start of the rainy season in Brazil. Crocodilians often come together in loose groups, for example when basking, nesting or sharing food. The largest, oldest crocodiles dominate the group. Scent glands on a crocodile's jaw and under its tail produce smells that tell the other crocodiles its place in the pecking order. The younger ones steer clear, resting at the fringes of the basking area and avoiding their elders when they are in the water.

143

Courting Crocodiles

Crocodilians are sociable animals throughout the year, but during the mating season, more communication than usual takes place. Males jostle to become the dominant animal in their stretch of river. They need to establish their social position because the dominant male will mate with most of the females in his territory. Females also need to indicate to the male that they wish to mate.

Courtship behavior for both male and female crocodilians includes bellowing and grunting, rubbing heads and bodies, blowing bubbles, circling and riding on the partner's back.

▲ POT NOSE

Most male gharials have a strange bump, or pot, on the end of the snout near the nostrils. Females have flat snouts. No one is quite sure what the pot is for, but it is probably used in courtship. It may help the male to change hissing sounds into buzzing sounds as air vibrates inside the hollow pot.

◄ TOUCHING COUPLE

Crocodilians touch each other a lot during courtship, especially around the head and neck. Males try to impress females by bubbling water from the nostrils and mouth. An interested female arches her back, then raises her head with her mouth open. The two may push each other under the water to see how big and strong their partner is.

144

◄ SWEET-SMELLING SCENT

Crocodilians have little bumps under their lower jaws. These are called musk glands. The musk is a sweet-smelling, greenish, oily perfume. It produces a scent that attracts the opposite sex. Musk glands are more noticeable in male crocodilians. During courtship, the male may rub his throat across the female's head and neck. This releases the scent from the musk glands and helps to prepare the female for mating.

FIGHTING MALES ►

Male crocodilians may fight each other for the chance to court and mate with females. They may spar with their jaws open or make themselves look bigger and more powerful by puffing up their bodies with air. Saltwater crocodiles are particularly violent and bash their heads together with a loud thud. These contests may go on for an hour or more but do not seem to cause much permanent damage.

◄ THE MATING GAME

A female crocodile often begins the courtship process. She approaches the male and raises her head, exposing her vulnerable throat to show she is no threat. She rubs against the male's head and neck, nudging and pushing him gently. Courtship can last for up to two hours before mating occurs. Both male and female crocodiles court and mate with several different partners.

Feuding Birds of Prey

Birds often squabble over food, and birds of prey (raptors) are no exception. Some birds of prey intimidate others that have already made a kill and try to force them to drop it. This behavior is called piracy. Sometimes birds of prey are attacked by the birds that they prey on. A number of small birds may join forces against a larger adversary and give chase, usually calling loudly. This is known as mobbing and it generally serves to confuse and irritate the raptor and also warns other prey in the area.

Birds of prey must also defend their nests against predators. The eggs and chicks of ground-nesting raptors are especially vulnerable to attack. Nesting adults will often fly at intruders and try to chase them off.

▲ SCRAP IN THE SNOW
On the snowy shores of the Kamchatka Peninsula, in northeast Russia, these sea eagles are fighting over a fish. A Steller's sea eagle, the biggest of all sea eagles, is shown on the right, with its huge wings outstretched. Its opponents, struggling in the snow, are white-tailed eagles. The two kinds of sea eagles are bound to meet and fight, because they occupy a similar habitat and feed on similar prey—fish, birds and small mammals.

◀ FISH FIGHT
Two common buzzards fight over a dead fish they have both spotted. Buzzards do not go fishing themselves, but they will feed on any carrion they find.

common buzzards
(Buteo buteo)

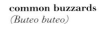

146

UNDER THREAT ▶

On the plains of Africa, a dead animal carcass attracts not only vultures, but other scavengers as well. Here, a jackal is trying to get a look, but a lappet-faced vulture is warning it off with outstretched wings.

Did you know? Hunters once used eagle owls as bait to attract mobbing birds into range.

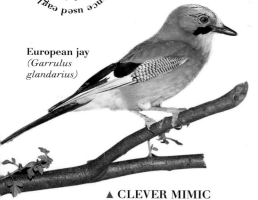

European jay
(*Garrulus glandarius*)

▲ CLEVER MIMIC

When a jay spots a predator, such as a bird of prey, it gives out an alarm call or mimics the predator's own call to warn other jays.

▲ IN HOT PURSUIT

An osprey has seen this pelican dive into the water and assumes that it now has a fish in its pouch. So it gives chase. Time and again, the osprey will fly straight at the pelican and scare it so much that it will finally release the fish from its pouch.

▼ MOB RULE

A number of crows have ganged up to mob a steppe eagle. They are bold enough to perch dangerously close to their enemy, calling loudly to persuade it to move on. Although the eagle would be more than a match for its tormentors, it might fly off just to escape aggravation.

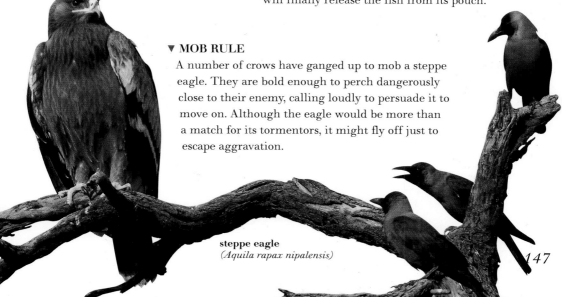

steppe eagle
(*Aquila rapax nipalensis*)

147

Close Raptor Couples

Most birds of prey stay with their mates for life. However, every year, during the breeding time, the pair strengthen their bonds with each other. This process is called courting.

In courtship displays there is usually a great deal of calling to each other, with the birds close together. The male may offer the female prey that he has caught. This shows her that he is an able hunter and can provide food for her when she is brooding (sitting on eggs) and also provide for their chicks.

Since most birds of prey are superb fliers, however, the most spectacular courtship displays take place in the air. The birds may perform acrobatic dances, or fly side by side, then swoop at each other and even clasp talons. The male may also drop prey while in flight for the female to dive and catch in an extravagant game of courtship feeding.

▲ **THE MARRIED COUPLE**
Like most birds of prey, American bald eagles usually mate for life. They occupy the same nest year after year, gradually adding to it each time they return to breed.

◄ **TOGETHERNESS**
Secretary birds become inseparable for life once they have paired up, rarely straying apart. Their courtship flights are most impressive, as they fly through the sky with their long tails streaming behind them. They also sleep side by side in their nest throughout the year, not just during the breeding season.

▲ A MOUSE FOR A MATE

A male barn owl has caught a mouse and takes it to his mate back in the nest. This behavior is called courtship feeding. It helps strengthen the bond between the pair. It is also preparation for the time when the female is nest-bound and incubating their eggs.

▼ BALANCING ACT

A pair of ospreys struggle to keep their balance as they mate on a high perch. The male scrunches up his feet to avoid hurting the female with his talons. Ospreys generally pair for life, but if mating is unsuccessful, they will "divorce."

▲ CARACARAS ON DISPLAY

A pair of striated caracaras call to one another by their nest. They are no longer courting but are raising their young. Mated pairs display like this frequently in order to strengthen the bond between them.

Did you know? Peregrines spend hours performing an amazing courtship flight.

osprey
(Pandion haliaetus)

▲ FACE TO FACE

A pair of Egyptian vultures stand face to face on the ground as part of an elaborate courtship display. In addition to their ground-based performances, the pair will also perform spectacular aerial displays. They fly, climb and dive close together, often presenting their talons to each other.

149

Herds of Horses

Horses, like zebras and asses, are herd animals, and horses living in the wild form what is described as a "stable" herd. Each member of the herd knows everyone else. The groups are strictly structured, with each animal knowing its place. Stable herds consist of a single stallion with a collection of mares and their foals. The group of mares is called a harem.

Wild asses and Grevy's zebras have a loose, or "unstable" herd structure. They live in dry habitats where individual dominant males defend territories that contain water and food. Females live in unstable groups, usually with related animals. They enter the territories of resident males to feed and drink, and so the males will join their herds on a temporary basis.

▲ LEARNING BEHAVIOR
A foal learns its first lessons on survival from its mother. In a process called imprinting, foals bond to the animal they see most often, which is usually their mother, within a few days of being born. They later learn from watching other members of the herd.

BACHELOR BOYS ▶
These young males have been driven from their herd. At two to three years, they are old enough to form a threat to the reigning stallion. Lone male horses find survival difficult away from the herd. Like these three, they often form small herds called bachelor groups.

◄ SOCIAL RISE
Like horses, plains zebras live in a stable herd. Each zebra has its position in the pecking order. Zebras are very sociable animals. They groom one another by nuzzling each other's manes and withers (shoulders) with their front teeth.

▲ HERD ORDER
This group of wild horses is a typical herd, consisting of a dominant stallion, six mares and a foal. The foal will have the same social status as its mother until it grows up. It moves up the social ladder as it gains more experience.

FEMALE POWER ►
Mares and stallions take different roles in the herd. It is usually the dominant mare who decides where to graze and when to move on. The stallion keeps the group together and prevents mares from leaving the herd.

◄ SEASONAL CHANGE
Herds do not always remain the same size. These wild asses live in the desert. When food is scarce they live in small groups, but during the wet season they gather in larger groups of up to 50.

151

Horse Language

Because horses are sociable animals that live in herds, they need to communicate with each other. They have a wide range of expressive behavior ranging from sounds and smells to a complex body language.

Animals recognize each other by their appearance and smell, and certain sounds are common to all equids. The short whinny is a warning call, while the long version is a sign of contentment. Other calls, such as greetings and aggressive threats, vary from species to species. Horses whinny, asses bray, mountain zebras whistle, and plains zebras bark. Horses, asses and zebras recognize and react to the calls of all other species of equids but do not respond to the calls of cattle or antelope.

▲ ON YOUR GUARD!
Horses need to work out where they fit in the social order of the herd. This horse has flattened its ears in a threatening posture—it is showing its dominance. Flattened ears can also indicate boredom or tiredness.

▲ BABY TALK
Young horses show respect to their elders by holding their ears to the side, displaying their teeth and making chewing movements. This is not a sign that the foal might bite, but is rather like preparing for a mutual grooming session. It's a way of saying "I'm friendly."

▲ TAKING NOTE
Horses are alert to the signals of others. If one horse is curious about something, its ears will prick forwards. The rest of the herd will look to see what has caught its interest.

◄ MUTUAL GROOMING

Horses, like all other equids, will nibble a favorite partner, grooming those places they cannot reach for themselves. The amount of time two horses spend grooming each other shows how friendly they are. Grooming helps to keep a herd together, and it occurs even when the horses' coats are in perfect condition.

FRIENDLY GREETING ►

When members of a herd meet up, they welcome each other with a series of greeting rituals. They may stretch heads, touch and sniff noses, push each other and then part. Good friends may lay their heads on each other's back.

◄ WILD AT HEART

Mares often develop personal bonds with other horses in the herd. These bonds can form between unrelated mares or with close relatives, such as sisters or adult daughters. The bonds are stronger in all-female herds. In groups led by a stallion, the mares make him their center of attention. The stallion may have a favorite mare, which he spends a lot of time with.

Elephant Families

An elephant family group is made up of related females and their offspring. Each family is led by an older, dominant female known as the matriarch. She makes all the decisions for the group. Bulls (male elephants) leave their family group when they are between 10 and 16 years old. When they are adults, only the strongest males mate with the females. Bulls spend most of their lives in small, all-male groups or wander on their own. Each family group has close links with up to five other families in the same area. These linked groups make up a herd. An elephant's day follows a regular pattern of feeding, sleeping and traveling to new feeding areas. Meeting, greeting and communicating with other elephants is an important part of every day and interrupts other activities from time to time. Adult elephants cooperate with each other to protect and guide the young.

▲ KEEPING IN TOUCH

A group of elephants drink together. The calves stay close to the group, so that they are continually touched by their mothers, or other close relatives, for reassurance.

▼ FOLLOW MY LEADER

Touch is a vital tool in elephant communication. As the group moves together, they constantly touch each other. In this way, the matriarch controls when they eat, drink and rest. She also protects the group from dangers and controls family members who misbehave.

sire bull
(male parent)

young bulls

juveniles

infants   adult sisters/daughters   matriarch

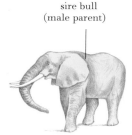

▲ AFRICAN ELEPHANTS

A family of African
elephants usually consists
of a matriarch, her adult
daughters and sisters, their
calves and a number of
young males and females.
Bulls may sometimes join
the family for mating but
they do not stay with it for
long. They soon leave to
resume their solitary lives.

◄ SMALL GROUPS

Elephants in Asia
live in smaller
groups than African
elephants. Asian
families have
between four and
eight members,
although as many as
10–20 individuals
may stay in touch.

◄ ALL ALONE

Male elephants do
not form such
strong social bonds
with each other as
the females in
family groups do.
As a result, some
bulls lead entirely
solitary lives.
However, their calls
carry over such a
range that it seems
likely that, even
when out of each
other's sight, most
bull elephants
remain in
long-distance
communication.

Communicating Elephants

Everyone knows the loud trumpeting sound that elephants make. They make this noise when they are excited, surprised, angry or lost. Elephants also make a wide range of low, rumbling sounds that carry for many miles through forests and grasslands. Different rumbles might mean "Where are you?" or "Let's go" or "I want to play." Females can signal when they are ready to mate, and family members can warn each other of danger.

But sound is just one way in which elephants can communicate with one another. They also touch, smell, give off chemical signals and perform visual displays, by altering the positions of the ears and the trunk. Their sense of smell can even tell them about another elephant's health.

▲ ELEPHANT GREETING
When elephants meet, they touch each other with their trunks, smell each other and rumble greeting sounds. Frightened elephants also touch others for reassurance.

BODY LANGUAGE ▶
Elephants send visual signals by moving their ears and trunk. Spreading the ears wide makes the elephant look bigger. This sends a message to a potential attacker to stay away. The elephant also stands up extra tall to increase the threat, raising its tusks, shaking its head and flapping its ears.

Did you know? Humans can only hear about one-third of the sounds an elephant makes.

◄ TRUNK CALL

An elephant makes its familiar high-pitched trumpeting call. Elephants also make a variety of crying, bellowing, screaming, snorting and rumbling sounds. Asian elephants make sounds that African elephants do not, and many of their rumbles last for longer. There are over 20 different kinds of rumble, with females making many more rumbling sounds than males. Females sometimes make rumbling calls when they are together, but male elephants do not do this.

▲ ALARM SIGNALS

This nervous baby elephant is interested in the crocodiles lying on the river bank. It raises its ears, either in alarm or as a threat to the crocodiles. If a baby calls out in distress, its relatives rush to its side, with rumbles of reassurance and comforting touches with their trunks.

▲ TOUCH AND SMELL

An elephant's skin is very sensitive, and touch is an important way of communicating feelings in elephant society. Smells also pass on useful messages, such as when a female or male is ready to mate.

Babar

One of the most famous elephants in children's literature is Babar the elephant king. He was created by French writer Jean de Brunhoff. Babar rules over the Land of the Elephants with the help of his wife Queen Celeste and his old friend General Cornelius. He fights wars with the rhinos, escapes from the circus and has many other exciting adventures.

Bear Aggression

Adult bears are solitary animals. They prefer to wander alone and do not like other bears. When two animals do meet they need to establish which is the dominant one. This sometimes means a fight, but usually it is just a shouting match and display. If one bear can scare away the other without a fight, it means there is less chance of either animal being injured.

Some bears do congregate together in one area at certain times of year, but this is to take advantage of a plentiful food source. Brown bears tolerate each other at fishing rivers and polar bears scavenge together at whale carcasses and rubbish dumps. As soon as the food is gone, the bears resume their solitary life.

▲ STAND TALL
To show aggression, bears rear on their hind legs, as this American black bear is doing. This makes it look bigger and more frightening. The bear will also growl at its opponent and show its teeth.

◄ ICE DANCE
Like two ballet dancers, young male polar bears play at fighting. They use exaggerated lunges and swipes with their paws and jaws. They do not hurt each other, but they must learn to fight well. Later in life as fully grown adults they will compete with other males for females during the breeding season. Fights between well-matched individuals can be violent and often bloody.

The Jungle Book
Rudyard Kipling's famous story The
Jungle Book *was first published in
1894. A young boy named Mowgli
is brought up by wolves. He is
befriended by Baloo the bear and
Bagheera the panther, who teach him
the law of the jungle. The tiger Shere
Khan plots to kill the man-cub.*

▲ TRAGEDY ON THE ICE
Adult male polar bears are cannibals. They will kill
cubs and feed upon the body. Here a female has
attacked and driven away the male, but her cub is
unlikely to survive. Male bears are much bigger than
females, but a female with cubs is a fierce opponent.

▲ FRIENDS AT THE FEAST
Brown bears gather to catch salmon in
Alaska. They use body language, such as
ears pointed forward or back, necks
stretched or contracted, to avoid conflicts
and establish the pecking order.

▲ FISHING BREAK
Young brown bears take a break from learning to
fish and practice fighting instead. They fight by
pushing and shoving at each other, using their
enormous bulk to overcome their opponent. They
also try to bite each other around the head and neck.

Big Cat Signals

Although most big cats are solitary, they do communicate with one another. They indicate how old they are, whether they are male or female, what mood they are in and where they live. Cats communicate by signals such as smells, scratches and sounds. The smells come from urine and from scent glands. Cats have scent glands on their heads and chins, between their toes and at the base of their tails. Every time they rub against something, they transfer their special smell. Cats make many different sounds. Scientists know that cats speak to each other, but still do not understand much about their language. Cats also communicate using body language. They use their ears to signal their mood and twitch their tails to show if they are excited or agitated.

▲ A MIGHTY ROAR
The lion's roar is the loudest sound cats make. It is loud enough for all the neighborhood lions to hear. Lions roar after sunset, following a kill and when they have finished eating. Lions make at least nine different sounds. They also grunt to each other as they move around.

HISSING LEOPARD ▶
An angry leopard hisses at an enemy. Cats hiss and spit when they feel threatened, or when they are fighting an enemy. The position of a cat's ears also signals its intentions. When a cat is about to attack, it flattens its ears back against its neck.

▲ EAR SIGNALS

Many wild cats, such as this tiger, have white markings on the back of their ears. They turn their ears to show the markings to an enemy when they are angry.

▲ MARKS FOR SHOW

Cats like to scratch things to clean their claws and stretch their limbs. At the same time they leave a scented mark for others to both see and smell. When this lioness scratches, she leaves her own personal scent from the glands between her toes on the scratch marks.

▲ CAT SPRAY

A king cheetah marks its territory by spraying urine at points along its trails. Scent marks left by a male tell other males to stay away. The scent left by a female will tell a nearby male if she is ready to mate.

BABY TALK ▶

Mothers talk to their cubs a lot. The sounds are quiet so that enemies do not hear. The softest and safest sound of all is purring.

Did you know? When they are close together, lions chirrup, meow and yowl to each other.

Life in a

Lions live in family groups called prides. A pride may contain 30 or 40 animals consisting of up to 12 lionesses and their cubs and three or four adult males, but many prides may be much smaller. Each pride defends its territory and does not allow other lions to hunt there. Lionesses usually stay in the same pride until they die, but male cubs are driven out when they are about three years old. They roam in small groups called coalitions until they are fully grown. Each coalition attempts to take over an existing pride by killing or driving out the old males.

FATHER AND SON

Male lions are the only big cats that look different from the females. Their long, shaggy manes make them look larger and fiercer and protect their necks in a fight. A male cub starts to grow a mane at about the age of three, he is then driven out of the pride and must establish his own territory.

FAMILY MEETING

A large pride of lions rests near a waterhole. When members of the pride meet, they greet each other with soft moans, swinging their heads from side to side and holding their tails high. Then they head-butt.

Lion Pride

NURSERY SCHOOL
Young lions play tag to learn how to chase things and to defend their pride. The pride does not usually allow strange lions to join the family group. Young lions need to be prepared in case other lions come to fight with them.

FIRST AT THE TABLE
Male lions usually eat first, even though the females do most of the hunting. Lions are the only cats that share their feast. All other cats kill prey and eat alone.

CAT SCRAP
Two lionesses fight each other to decide who will be the first to eat. There is usually a dominant female in each pride, even when there are males around. This chief female rules the family.

MOTHER AND CUBS
Lionesses give birth to a litter of between one and six cubs. Male cubs stay with their mother for over two years and the females usually stay for a lifetime. The mother calls her cubs to her with a soft growl and they respond.

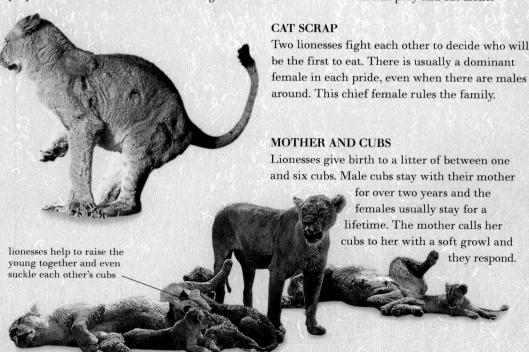

lionesses help to raise the young together and even suckle each other's cubs

Cat Communication

The social lions are the exception among big cats. Most cats lead solitary lives. They hunt alone and the females bring up their cubs alone. Big cats come together only when they want to mate. Their loner lifestyle has evolved because of their need to find food. There is usually not enough prey in one area for a large group of big cats to live on.

All wild cats have territories that they defend from other cats. These areas will include a hunting area, drinking places, lookout positions and (for females) a den where she brings up her young. Female cats have smaller territories than males. Males that have more than one mate have territories that overlap with two or more female territories.

Did you know? Big cats' territories range from a few miles to over 620 miles.

▲ **BRINGING UP BABY**

Female snow leopards bring up their cubs on their own. They have up to five cubs who stay with their mother for at least a year. Although snow leopards are loners, they are not unsociable. They like to live near each other and let other snow leopards cross their territories.

◄ **THE LOOKOUT**

A puma keeps watch over its territory from a hill. Pumas are solitary and deliberately avoid each other except during courtship and mating. The first male puma to arrive in an area claims it as his territory. He chases out any other male that tries to live there.

▲ A PRIDE OF LIONS
The lions in a pride drink together, hunt together, eat together and play together. They try to avoid contact with other prides. To tell the others to keep out of its territory, the pride leaves scent markings on the edge of its range.

Daniel and the Lions' Den
A story in the Bible tells how Daniel was taken prisoner by Nebuchadnezzar, king of Babylon. When Daniel correctly interpreted the king's dreams he became the king's favorite. His enemies became jealous of his position and had him thrown into a lions' den, a common punishment for prisoners at the time. But instead of eating Daniel, the lions befriended him. They were tamed by his great faith in God.

▲ FAMILY GROUPS
A cheetah mother sits between her two cubs. The cubs will leave their mother at about 18 months old and the female then lives alone. Males, however, live in small groups and defend a territory. Male cheetahs are the only big cats apart from lions to live in groups.

▲ WELL GROOMED
Cats that live together groom each other. They do this to be friendly and to keep clean. Cats also groom to spread their scent on each other, so that they smell the same. This helps them to recognize each other and identify strangers.

The Communities of Wolves

Wolves are very social animals. A few may live alone, but most live in packs. Most wolf packs have between 8 and 24 members. The main purpose of living in a pack is to hunt. A team of wolves working together can hunt down and kill much larger and stronger prey than a solitary wolf could. Only the strongest, healthiest pair in the wolf pack will actually mate. Every pack member then helps to feed and bring up the cubs.

Other canids have a similar social structure. Bush dogs, dholes and African hunting dogs also live in packs, while jackals, and sometimes coyotes and raccoon dogs, live in smaller family groups. Maned wolves and foxes usually live alone and prey on smaller animals.

▲ TWO'S COMPANY
A pair of jackals drink from a water hole in South Africa. Most jackals pair up for life and cooperate over rearing their pups. Jackals also work together when hunting. They use yips, growls, hisses and howls to work together to hunt down their prey.

Did you know?
Foxes produce alarming screams when looking for a mate.

ON PATROL ▶
A wolf pack is led by the strongest, most experienced animals. Every morning the pack patrols the edges of its territory, making fresh scent markings and checking for strange scents that will tell them if rival wolves have been there.

maned wolf
(*Chrysocyon
brachyurus*)

▲ A FAMILY AFFAIR

Dholes live in family packs of between
five and twelve animals. Sometimes
several families join together to form a
large dhole pack called a clan. Hunting
in a big group helps these relatively
small wild dogs to tackle large prey
such as wild cattle and buffalo.

▲ EACH FOR ITSELF

The maned wolf is mostly solitary, living and hunting
rodents on its own. It does not howl, but barks, whines
and yaps like a domestic dog. It also growls when it is
frightened or preparing to attack.

◄ COYOTE COUPLE

Most coyotes live and
hunt alone, in pairs or
in small family units.
Coyotes mark their
territory with urine or
feces. The smell warns
intruders that another
coyote is living here and
to stay away.

DOG SOCIETY ►

African hunting dogs are
the next most social canids
after wolves, and hunt
cooperatively. Unlike most
other canids, however,
African hunting dogs are
not territorial and do not
make scent markings with
their urine.

Living in

A wolf pack has a strict social order and each member knows its place. The senior male and female, known as the alpha male and female, are the only animals to breed. The alpha male takes the lead in hunting, defends the pack members from enemies, and keeps the other animals in their place. In most packs, a second pair of wolves, called the beta male and female, come next in the ranking order. The other pack members are usually the offspring of the alpha pair, aged up to three years old.

LEADER OF THE PACK
An alpha male wolf greets a junior pack member. Wolves use different body positions and facial expressions to show rank. The leader stands upright with tail held high. The junior has his ears laid back and his tail tucked between his legs.

IT'S A PUSHOVER
A junior wolf rolls over on its back in a gesture of submission to a more dominant pack member. A junior wolf can also pacify a stronger animal by imitating cub behavior, such as begging for food.

SHOWING WHO IS BOSS
A wolf crouches down to an alpha male. The young wolf whines as it cowers, as if to say, "You're the boss." The pack leader's confident stance makes him look as large as possible.

a Wolf Pack

"I GIVE UP"

A male gray wolf lays its ears back and sticks its tongue out. Taken together, these two gestures signal submission. A wolf with its tongue out, but its ears pricked, is sending a different message, showing it feels hostile and rebellious.

REJECTED BY THE PACK

Old, wounded or sickly wolves are often turned out of the pack to become lone wolves. Although pack members may be affectionate with each other, there is no room for sentiment. Young wolves may also leave to start their own packs. Lone wolves without the protection of a pack are much more vulnerable to attack and must be more cautious.

SCARY SNARL

A gray wolf bares its canine teeth in a snarl of aggression. Studies have shown that wolves use up to 20 different facial expressions. Junior wolves use snarling expressions to challenge the authority of their leaders. The alpha male may respond with an even more ferocious snarl. If it does so, the junior wolf is faced with a choice. It must back down, or risk being punished with a nip.

169

Primates Living Together

All primates communicate in some way with other members of their species, and most of them live in social groups. Community living has advantages. There are more eyes to spot predators, and several animals can work as a team to fight off attack or forage for food. As a community, they stand a better chance of survival if there is a problem with the food supply, during a drought, for instance. The leaders will feed themselves and their young first to make sure that they survive. Solitary animals may have a hard time finding a mate, but within a group, there's plenty of choice. And, when there are young to be cared for, a community can provide many willing helpers.

Nocturnal prosimians rely on being solitary and silent to avoid being noticed by predators. Among bush babies and lorises, even couples live independently of each other, but they occupy the same patch, and their paths often cross. Babies stay with their mother until they are old enough to live alone.

▲ TREE-SHARING
Sifakas work together in groups of about seven adults to defend their territory. They are generally led by the females, and males may switch groups.
These prosimians gather in the higher branches of the trees in western Madagascar. If danger threatens, they all start a hiccuping groan.

HAPPY COUPLE ►
In the jungles of South America, male and female sakis mate and usually live as a couple for a year. The female cares for the young. The father may not spend the day with his family, but does return to them at night. If there is plenty of food, families mingle with each other, forming large, loosely knit groups.

◄ FEMALE RULE

A female is in charge of this troop of black tufted-ear marmosets. As with most other New World marmosets and tamarins, there may be several other females, but only the head female breeds. She mates with all the males to make sure her top-level genes are passed on. As none of the males know who is the father, they all help rear and protect the young.

EQUAL SOCIETY ►

The relationship between a woolly monkey mother and her children can last for life. Woolly monkeys live in troops — there may be 20 to 50 of them, with roughly equal numbers of males and females. Adult males often cooperate, and all the males and females can mate with each other. Individual females care for their own young. Woolly monkey groups are bound by an intricate web of relationships between all members that is hard for outsiders to understand.

◄ MALE POWER

These female hamadryas baboons are just two in a harem of several females. A single, top male mates with all the females to make sure he fathers all the children. Males with no harem live in separate bachelor groups of two or three. They try to mate with a harem when the leader is not looking. When the leader gets old, a few young males will team up to depose him. Once he has been chased away, the victors fight for control of the harem.

Monkey Signals

Attracting attention in a noisy forest is a challenge. Groups of tree-living monkeys and prosimians lose sight of each other and keep in touch by calling. Nocturnal prosimians, however, need to keep a low profile, and so they leave scent messages that are easier to place accurately.

All prosimians and, to a lesser extent, monkeys, send messages of ownership, aggression or sexual readiness with strong-smelling urine or scent from special glands. Monkeys can also express their feelings with facial expressions and gestures, and some use their ability to see in color. African guenons, for example, have brightly colored patches on their bodies that can be seen by their companions when they are hurtling through the trees. Even fur and tails can be useful. Ring-tailed lemurs swish their tails menacingly at rivals, and at the same time, fan evil smells over them.

▲ DON'T HURT ME

This toque macaque is showing by its posture and expression that it is no threat. If an adult monkey wants to make friends, it may make a sound like a human baby gurgling. The other monkey will usually respond gently.

Did you know? Monkeys have more face muscles and make more expressions than prosimians.

PERSONAL PERFUME ▶

A black spider monkey smears a strong-smelling liquid on a branch. The liquid is produced by a gland on the monkey's chest. Its smell is unique to this monkey. When other monkeys smell it, they know that another of their kind has been there. If they meet the particular monkey that left the scent, they will recognize it.

In complicated langur societies, high-ranking males hold their tails higher than lesser members of the group. Primates that live in complex social groups have a wider range of communication skills than solitary species. More information has to be passed around among a greater number of individuals.

▲ YOU SCRATCH MY BACK . . .
Grooming a fellow monkey not only gets rid of irritating fleas and ticks, but also forges a relationship. A lot of monkey communication is about preventing conflicts among group members. Forming strong personal bonds hold the troop together.

▲ BE CAREFUL
A mandrill has mobile face muscles to make different expressions. Here, he pulls back his gums and snarls. This makes him look very menacing to other males.

▲ I'M ANGRY
When a mandrill becomes angry, he opens his mouth in a wide yawn to show the size of his teeth and roars. Another monkey will hesitate before confronting this male.

LOOKING FIERCE ►
This marmoset is literally bristling for a fight. Its fur stands on end like an angry cat's to make it look much bigger. It may scare its rival into withdrawing. Marmosets look cute, but they squabble a lot among themselves.

Ape Groups

Of all the apes, chimpanzees live in the largest groups—up to about 100 individuals. The chimps constantly change their friends and often drop out altogether to spend time on their own. A chimpanzee group is based around the most important male chimps. Gorilla groups are similar but smaller, led by a strong adult male called a silverback. Bonobos live in smaller groups than chimpanzees, but their society is led by females rather than males. Orangutans tend to live on their own, although females and their young spend a lot of time together while the youngster is growing up. Gibbons have a completely different social system from that of other apes – they live in family groups of a mother, father and their young.

▲ GENTLE GIANTS
Life in a gorilla group is generally friendly and there is seldom serious fighting within the group. The silverback (named for the white hair on its back) can stop most squabbles by strutting and glaring at the troublemakers. He is the group's leader, deciding where it will travel and where it will settle.

Did you know? Bonobos can understand human language as well as a toddler.

bonobos
(*Pan paniscus*)

▼ SOCIABLE SOCIETY
Bonobos are very sociable creatures. Most of the time they live in large, loose groups, called communities, which are split up into smaller groups of 15 or less when foraging for food.

juvenile male

male silverback leader

adult female

young gorilla

◄ HAPPY FAMILIES

Gorillas like to live in extended family groups, usually with between five and thirty members. A gorilla without a group will do its best to join one or start a new one. Each group is controled and defended by a silverback.

LONE ORANG ▶

Orangutans spend most of their time alone. One reason for this may be that they need to eat a lot of fruit every day. If lots of orangutans lived together, they would not be able to find enough fruit to eat. Even when they do meet, they often ignore each other.

▲ TREETOP SINGERS

Gibbons live in family groups and are the only apes to mate for life. A mated pair of gibbons "sing" a loud duet to declare their territory to other gibbons in the forest. The male hoots, whoops and wails, while the female makes a rising twitter.

BEST FRIENDS ▶

Females form the backbone of a bonobo group. Adult female bonobos form strong friendships, which are reinforced by grooming and hugging each other. This group of female bonobos have been raised in captivity. Boredom in captivity leads some apes to pluck out their hair.

bonobos
(Pan paniscus)

Great Ape Language

▼ GIBBON DUET
As well as warning other gibbons to stay out of their territories, the duet sung by gibbon pairs may also help to strengthen the bond between them. The pair will also use facial expressions to show feelings such as fear and excitement.

Although apes cannot speak, they communicate with a variety of sounds, facial expressions and gestures. Scientists have even learned some of this ape-speak in order to reassure the apes they are studying, and avoid frightening the animals away. Orangutans and gibbons both call loudly to stake their claim to their territory, rather as we would put up a fence and a "keep out" sign around our property. In chimp and gorilla societies, body positions and gestures show which animals are most important, or dominant, and which are least important, or submissive. Chimps and gorillas also communicate through a variety of sounds, especially chimps, who can be very noisy apes.

siamang gibbon
(*Hylobates syndactylus*)

▲ MAKING FACES
Chimpanzees have a variety of different expressions for communication. A wide, open and relaxed mouth is a play face used to start, or during, a game. An angry chimp clenches its lips shut.

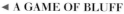

◄ A GAME OF BLUFF

Rising on his back legs, a male silverback gorilla slaps his cupped hands rapidly against his chest, making a "pok-pok-pok" sound. Then he charges forward, tearing up plants and slapping the ground. This display is really a bluff to scare away rivals. Gorillas hardly ever fight, and a male usually stops his charge at the last minute.

▲ GORILLA-SPEAK

Researchers observing gorillas in the wild have learned to make the same sounds and gestures as the gorillas. A content gorilla makes a rumbling belch sound. A sharp, pig-grunt noise means the gorilla is annoyed.

◄ KEEP OUT!

Fully grown male orangutans usually keep to a particular area of forest – up to 6 square miles. This is called their home range. Every day, a male roars loudly to warn other orangutans to stay away. This long call lasts for about two minutes. By calling, males avoid meetings that might end in a fight.

TOP CHIMP ►

The dominant chimpanzee in a group shows off occasionally by charging about, screaming and throwing branches. He also hunches his shoulders and makes his hair stand up on end.

▼ LOW RANK

To avoid fighting with important chimps, low-ranking chimps behave in a certain way. They flatten their hair, crouch down or bob up and down, and back towards the more important chimp, while pant-grunting.

The Close

All the chimpanzees in a community know each other well. Mothers have a very strong bond with their young, and many chimps who are not related form close friendships, especially males. Dominant males form the stable core of a chimpanzee group and they will attack and even kill males from other communities. Female chimps may emigrate to a neighboring community. Members of a community will meet, spend time together and then separate throughout the day. In chimp society there is a hierarchy of importance, which is maintained by powerful males. The chimps jostle for position, constantly checking where they stand with each other and challenging their leaders.

YOU GROOM MY BACK

One of the most important activities in a chimpanzee group is grooming. It helps to keep the group together by allowing the chimps to strengthen friendships and patch up quarrels. High-ranking chimps are often groomed by low-ranking ones. It takes a young chimp about two years to learn how to groom properly.

MOTHERS AND BABIES

For the first three months of its life, a baby chimpanzee clings to its mother. By watching her face, it learns to copy her expressions of fear, anger and friendship. The bond between a mother chimpanzee and her young is very strong, and lasts for many years. In fact, the closest relationships within the family group are between a mother and her grown-up daughters.

Chimp Group

GANG WARFARE
A dominant male chimp often makes friends with two or three others, who spend time with him and back him up in fights. Powerful supporters enable a chimp to become a leader.

PLAYTIME
As young chimpanzees play, they get to know how to mix with the other chimps in a group. They learn how to greet others and which individuals are the most important.

FRIENDSHIP
To show their affection for one another, chimps hug, kiss and pat each other on the back. As males spend much more time together than females, this friendly contact is more common between males, although females strike up special friendships, too.

NOISY CHIMPS
Chimpanzees make more than 30 different sounds. When they are contented, they make soft "hooing" noises, when they discover food they hoot, and when they are excited they scream.

Whale Life

Many toothed whales—which eat fish and squid—are sociable and live together. Sperm whales live in groups of up to about 50. A group may be a breeding school of females and young or a bachelor school of young males. Older male sperm whales usually live alone. Beluga whales often live in groups of several hundred.

Baleen whales are not as sociable and move singly or in small groups. This is probably because they filter huge amounts of small creatures out of the water as they swim— they could not find enough food if they lived close together.

Did you know? Dolphins will nudge a sick member of the group up to the surface, so it does not drown.

▲ HERD INSTINCT

Beluga whales gather together in very large groups, or herds. They are noisy creatures whose voices can clearly be heard above the surface. This is why they are sometimes called sea canaries. Belugas have a wide range of facial expressions and often appear to be smiling.

▼ BONDED ORCAS

Two killer whales, or orcas, rise out of Antarctic waters together, as if on a signal. They are members of the same pod, or group, which stay together all their lives. The bonds between the animals are very strong. This helps them coordinate their activities, especially when they are hunting for food.

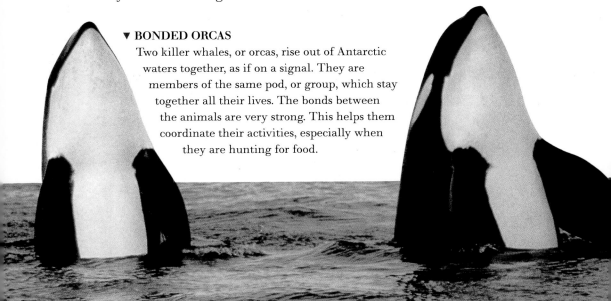

◀ STAYING CLOSE

Two Atlantic spotted dolphins swim with their young. Mother and young often play together, turning, rolling, and touching each other with their flippers. During play, the young dolphins learn the skills they need in later life.

▼ HUMAN CONTACT

A bottlenose dolphin swims alongside a boy. These dolphins usually live in social groups but lone animals often approach humans.

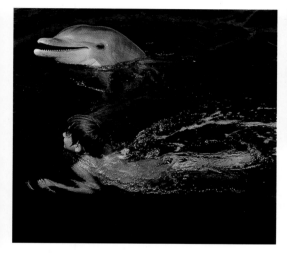

▲ SOLITARY SWIMMER

An Amazon river dolphin rests on the river bed. It spends most of its life alone, or with just one other. This solitary behavior is typical of river dolphins, but untypical of most ocean dolphins and whales.

HELP AT HAND ▶

These long-finned pilot whales are stranded on a beach. Pilot whales usually live in large groups, with strong bonds between group members. One whale may strand itself on a beach. If others try to help they may also get stranded.

Dolphins at Play

Dolphins delight people with their acrobatic antics. They somersault, ride the bow waves of boats and go surfing. Dusky and spinner dolphins are particularly lively. In most animal species only the young play. In whale and dolphin society, adults play too. Often the animals seem to perform just for fun. But some antics have a purpose, such as sending signals to other dolphins.

Dolphins also use whistles and clicking sounds to communicate. Each dolphin has a signature "whistle" to identify it. As each dolphin "talks" the other one listens.

▲ **PLAYFUL PAIR**
Two Atlantic spotted dolphins jostle as they play with a sea fan. Dolphins spend much of their time playing, especially the younger ones. They make up games, using anything they can find. Their games can last for many hours.

▼ **JUMPING FOR JOY**
A pair of bottlenose dolphins leap high, leaving the water together, as if they have rehearsed their act. They seem to jump for joy, but their behavior may have a social function within their family group.

▶ PORPOISING ON PURPOSE

A group of long-snouted spinner dolphins go porpoising, this is where they take long, low leaps as they swim. They churn the water behind them into a foam. Many dolphins practice porpoising, in order to travel fast on the surface.

Did you know? Killer whales like brushing against each other as they swim at high speed.

◀ RIDING THE WAKE

A Pacific white-sided dolphin surfs the waves. This is one of the most acrobatic of the dolphins, like other species of dolphins it likes to ride in the waves left in the wake of passing boats.

Did you know? The rough skin on a porpoise's back may be for giving calves piggy-back rides.

AQUATIC ACROBAT ▶

This dusky dolphin is throwing itself high into the air. It twists and turns, spins and performs somersaults. This behavior is like a roll call—to check that every dolphin in the group is present and ready to go hunting. The behavior is repeated after hunting to gather the group together once more.

Did you know? A dolphin may play cat and mouse with its prey before eating it.

The Sharks' Pecking Order

No shark is alone for very long. Sooner or later, one shark will come across another, including those of its own kind. In order to reduce the risk of fights and injury, sharks talk to each other, not with sound, but with body language. Sharks have a clear pecking order. The bigger the shark, the more important it is. Not surprisingly, small sharks tend to keep out of the way of larger ones. Many species use a sign that tells others to keep their distance. They arch their back, point their pectoral fins down and swim stiffly. If this doesn't work, the offending shark will be put in its place with a swift bite to the sides or head. Bite marks along its gill slits can be a sign that a shark has stepped out of line and been told firmly to watch out.

▲ **A COUPLE OF CHUMS**
Great white sharks were once thought to travel alone, but it is now known that some journey in pairs or small groups. Some sharks that have been identified by scientists will appear repeatedly at favorite sites, such as California's Farallon Islands, 26 miles off the coast of San Francisco. There they lie in wait for seals.

Did you know? Male sharks bite females to encourage them to mate.

◄ **BED FELLOWS**
Sharks, such as these whitetip reef sharks, will snooze alongside each other on the seabed. They search for a safe place to rest below overhanging rocks and coral, where, as fights rarely break out, they seem to tolerate each other. The sharks remain here until dusk, when they separate to hunt.

◄ ATTACK MARKS
This gray reef shark has swum too close to another, larger shark and has been bitten on its gill slits as a punishment. The marks on its skin show that its attacker raked the teeth of its lower jaw across the sensitive skin of the gray reef's gill slits. A shark's injuries heal rapidly, so this unfortunate victim will recover quickly from its wounds.

REEF SHARK GANGS ►
Sharks have their own personal space. When patrolling the edge of a reef, the blacktip reef sharks will tell others that they are too close by moving their jaw or opening their mouth. During feeding, order sometimes breaks down and a shark might be injured in the frenzy.

◄ SHARK SCHOOL
Every day schools of scalloped hammerhead sharks gather close to underwater mountains in the Pacific Ocean. They do not feed, even though they come across shoals of fish that would normally be food. Instead, they swim repeatedly up and down, as though taking a rest.

185

Schools for

By day scalloped hammerhead sharks swim in large groups called schools around underwater volcanoes in the Pacific, off the coast of Mexico, and the Cocos and Galapagos islands. This species of shark cannot stop swimming or it will drown, so schools are a safe resting place for them. Even sharks have enemies, such as other sharks and killer whales, and there is safety in numbers. In schools, scalloped hammerheads can also find a mate. At night, they separate to hunt. They swim to favorite feeding sites, they are thought to use their electric sensors to find their way.

BAD-TEMPERED SHARKS
The larger a female hammerhead becomes, the less likely she is to get on with her neighbors. Older and larger hammerhead sharks like more space than smaller, younger sharks. In hammerhead schools, the relationship between sharks seems to be controled by constant displays of threat and small fights.

FEMALES ONLY
The sharks in this huge school of hammerheads are mainly females. The larger sharks swim in the center and dominate the group, often butting one another to choose the best positions in which to swim. Not only is the middle safer, but it is also the place where the male sharks will be on the lookout for a mate.

Hammerheads

CLEAN UP OPERATION
At some gathering sites, such as Cocos Island in the eastern Pacific, sharks drop out of the school and swoop down to cleaning stations close to the reef. From the reef, butterfly fish dart out to eat the dead skin and irritating parasites that cling to the outside of the shark's body.

BODY LANGUAGE
Larger sharks within a school perform strange movements and dances to keep smaller sharks in their place. At the end of the movement, a large shark may nip a smaller one on the back of the head.

STRANGE HEAD
The scalloped hammerhead is so named because of the grooves along the front of its head, which gives it a scalloped (scooped out) appearance. The black tips on the underside of its pectoral fins are another way of identifying this shark.

New Life

Wild animals have developed a whole range of strategies to ensure
their offspring reach maturity and can breed themselves. Young
animals face danger from predators, the weather and starvation.
This section begins with pregnant mothers and follows the
offspring through to adulthood.

How Life Continues

The aim of all living things to reproduce more of their own kind. Most animals do this by sexual reproduction, and their young are a unique mix of their male and female parents. Sexual reproduction is successful because some of the young will combine the best elements of both their mother and father. These animals are better adapted to their environment and have the greatest chance of surviving.

The swallowtail butterfly does not stay with its young, but it ensures they have the best possible start in life. The eggs are well disguised and laid on a suitable food source, ready for when the caterpillars hatch.

Male and female animals

Most animals have two separate sexes—males and females. Males are often bigger than females, and male butterflies often have brighter colors than females. But the really important differences are in the internal organs. Males have testes that produce microscopic sperm, while the females have ovaries that produce eggs. A sperm and an egg join together in a process called fertilization to form a new animal.

Eggs or babies?

Most reptiles and birds form protective shells around their fertilized eggs and lay them as soon as possible. This means that the female is not burdened with a family of babies growing inside her. Female birds would find it impossible to fly if they gave birth to live young. On the other hand, the female has to provide each egg with a lot of food, in the form of a yolk, and this uses up a lot of her energy. Some snakes do give birth to live young, but their babies develop in a similar way, taking nourishment from the yolk of an egg. These snakes have decided that the safest nest site for their eggs is inside the mother's body.

This bear cub is a unique mix of its parents' genes. With any luck, it will have inherited the best characteristics from each. This will help it survive to produce cubs of its own—passing on the features that help it to survive in its environment.

Mammals have a different way of producing their young. Their eggs have no shells, and they grow into babies inside the female's body. The babies absorb food from their mother's blood. Carrying

Two female Atlantic spotted dolphins swim with their young. Dolphins are very sociable animals, and mothers and their young evidently enjoy each other's company.

babies inside the mother's body is a good way to protect them from danger, and it also means that the mother does not have to provide a lot of food at once. Only a few babies can be born at a time, but the mammals care for their young after birth so that they have the best possible chance of surviving to become new adults.

Parental care

Many animals abandon their eggs as soon as they have laid them. Predators eat a lot of these eggs and the newly hatched young, but parents make up for it by producing huge numbers of eggs. An insect may lay hundreds or even thousands of eggs. Animals that take good care of their eggs and their young lay far fewer eggs. Some insects and spiders, and all crocodiles, make good parents, finding food for their young or coming to their defence if danger threatens.

Baby mammals feed on milk from their mother's bodies for weeks, months or even years after birth. Many babies are naked and helpless when they are born, and they are fed and kept warm in a nest or den for several weeks. Horses and other grazing animals, however, give birth to well-developed babies that can get up and walk about immediately. These animals are always on the move, and a baby must be able to keep up with its mother. Mammals that give birth to large babies have one or perhaps two babies at a time, because of the limited room in a female's body.

Lions are fearsome predators, but when they are young they are in danger from other predators, such as hyenas and crocodiles. A cub's mother will guard it fiercely until it is large enough to defend itself.

The new generation

Each species of animal uses a slightly different strategy to ensure that at least some of their young survive. This book examines some of those strategies. You will discover how each animal tries to ensure its genes continue, so that at least one of its offspring goes on to breed itself.

A young chimpanzee is fully at home in the treetops. With attentive care from its mother and protection from its group, this young ape should survive to have offspring of its own.

The Transformation of a Beetle

▲ LAYING EGGS

A cardinal beetle lays her eggs in dead wood. The hard tip of the beetle's abdomen pierces the wood to lay the eggs inside. When the eggs hatch, the log provides the larvae with a hiding place from predators. They feast on wood-eating insects until they are fully grown.

Almost all insects start their lives as eggs. They go through dramatic life changes to become fully formed adults. When beetle larvae (grubs) hatch, they look nothing like their parents. Many resemble pale worms although some have legs. They often live in different places from adult beetles and may eat quite different food.

Larvae put most of their energy into finding food, and they eat constantly. They grow bigger but do not change form. When the larva is fully grown, it changes into a pupa. Inside the pupa, the grub's body dissolves and then rebuilds in a completely different shape. It emerges from the pupa stage as an adult beetle. This amazing four-stage process of change is called complete metamorphosis. The adult beetle is now ready to look for a mate, breed and create young.

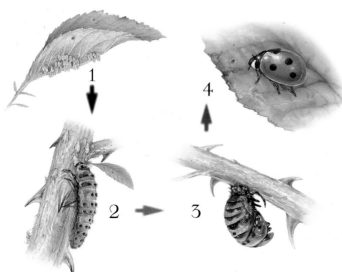

◄ ALL CHANGE

The ladybird's life cycle shows the four stages of complete metamorphosis. The adult lays eggs (1) and these hatch out into larvae or grubs (2). When fully grown, the larvae become pupae (3) before emerging as adult ladybirds (4). At each stage, the ladybird's appearance is totally different from the last, almost as if it were several animals in one.

◄ HIDDEN EGGS

These ladybird eggs have been glued on to a leaf so that they stand on end. Beetle eggs are generally round or oval, and they are usually yellow, green or black for camouflage. Eggs are usually laid in spring or summer, and most hatch between one and four weeks later. However, some eggs are laid in autumn and hatch the following spring, when there is plenty of food and conditions are warmer.

WRIGGLY LARVA ►

A cockchafer larva has a long, fat body that is very different from the adult's rounded shape. The larva does not have the long antennae or wings of the adult either, but unlike many beetle grubs, it does have legs. It moves about by wriggling its way through the soil.

◄ UNDER COVER

When a beetle grub is fully grown, it attaches itself to a plant stem or hides underground. Then it becomes a pupa, often with a tough outer skin. Unlike the grub, the pupa doesn't feed or move much. It looks dead, but inside an amazing change is taking place. The insect's body breaks down into a thick, soup-like liquid, and is then reshaped into an adult beetle.

PERFECTLY FORMED ADULT ►

A seven-spot ladybird struggles out of its pupa case. Like most adult beetles, it has wings, antennae and jointed legs. This ladybird's yellow wing cases will develop spots after just a few hours. Some beetles spend only a week as pupae before emerging as fully grown adults. Others pass the whole winter in the resting stage, waiting to emerge.

Caterpillar Survival

Like beetles, butterflies and moths go through a complete metamorphosis. They begin life as eggs, and hatch into caterpillars. At this stage they eat as much as possible, chomping their way through leaves, fruits and stems. They grow rapidly, shedding their skin several times as they swell. A caterpillar may grow to its full size within a month. Not all caterpillars reach the stage of becoming a chrysalis. Many are eaten by predators or killed by diseases. Caterpillars hide among vegetation and crevices in bark, often feeding at night to try to avoid danger.

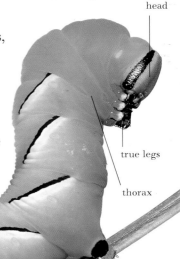

privet hawkmoth caterpillar
(Sphinx ligustri)

head

true legs

thorax

abdomen

this horn at the tip of the abdomen is typical of hawkmoth caterpillars

each proleg ends in a ring of hooks that are used to hold onto stems and leaves

the last pair of prolegs, called claspers, enable a caterpillar to cling very tightly to plants

◄ CATERPILLAR PARTS

Caterpillars have big heads with strong jaws for snipping off food. Their long, soft bodies are divided into 13 segments. The front three segments become the thorax in the adult insect and the rear segments become the abdomen.

FALSE LEGS ►

The caterpillar of an emperor gum moth has five pairs of prolegs (false legs) on its abdomen. All caterpillars have these prolegs, which help them cling on to plants. They lose the prolegs as an adult. Caterpillars also have three pairs of true legs, which become the legs of the adult.

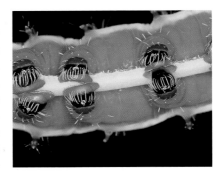

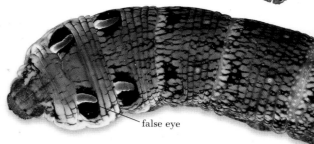

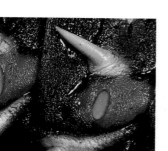

▲ BREATHING HOLES

A caterpillar does not have lungs for breathing like humans. Instead, it has tiny holes called spiracles that draw oxygen into the body tissues. There are several spiracles on each side of the caterpillar.

false eye

▲ FALSE EYES

The large eye shapes behind the head of an elephant hawkmoth caterpillar are actually false eyes for scaring predators. In fact, caterpillars can barely see at all. They possess six small eyes that can only distinguish between dark and light.

Did you know? Caterpillars can close up their spiracles and survive underwater for hours.

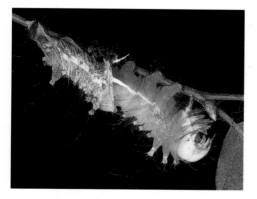

◄ CHANGING SKIN

Every week or so, the skin of a growing caterpillar grows too tight. It splits down the back to reveal a new skin underneath. At first, the new skin is soft and stretchy. As the caterpillar sheds its old skin, it swells the new one by swallowing air. It lies still for a few hours while the new large skin hardens. This skin changing process is called molting.

◄ FLY ATTACK

A puss moth caterpillar can defend itself against predators. It puffs up its front and whips its tail like a tiny dragon, before spraying a jet of poison over its foe.

SILK MAKERS ►

Peacock butterfly caterpillars live and feed in web-like tents. They spin these tents from silken thread. All caterpillars can produce this thread from a device called a spinneret under their mouth. The silk helps them to hold onto surfaces as they move.

195

the caterpillar's rear claspers grip a silken pad

The Birth

Once a caterpillar reaches its full size it is ready for the next stage in its metamorphosis, and it turns into a pupa or chrysalis. The caterpillars of many moths spin a silken cocoon around themselves before turning into pupae. Inside the chrysalis, the body parts of the caterpillar gradually dissolve. New features grow in their place, including a totally different head and body, and two pairs of wings. This whole process can take less than a week. When the changes are complete, almost magically, a fully formed adult emerges from the chrysalis.

1 The monarch butterfly caterpillar spins a silken pad onto a plant stem and grips it firmly with its rear claspers. It then sheds its skin to reveal the chrysalis (pupa), which clings to the silken pad with tiny hooks.

2 The chrysalis of the monarch butterfly is plump, pale and studded with golden spots. It appears lifeless except for the occasional twitch. However, changes can sometimes be vaguely seen through the skin.

the fully formed chrysalis

the chrysalis darkens before opening

3 The chrysalis grows dark and the wing pattern becomes visible just before the adult butterfly emerges. Inside, the insect pumps body fluids to its head and thorax (upper body). The chrysalis then cracks open behind the head and along the front of the wing.

# of a Butterfly

4 The butterfly swallows air to make itself swell up, which splits the chrysalis even more. The insect emerges shakily and clings tightly to the chrysalis skin.

the butterfly's wings are soft and crumpled at first

5 The newly emerged adult slowly pumps blood into the veins in its wings, which begin to straighten out. The insect hangs with its head up so that the force of gravity helps to stretch its wings. After about half an hour, the wings reach their full size.

split skin of the chrysalis

wing veins with blood pumping into them

6 The butterfly basks in the sun for an hour or two while its wings dry out and harden. After a few trial flaps of its wings, it is ready to fly away and begin life as an adult butterfly.

the bright color of the monarch butterfly warns predators that it is poisonous

monarch butterfly (*Danaus plexippus*)

Spider Eggs

Female spiders are usually larger than males because they need to carry a lot of eggs inside their bodies. The eggs are usually laid a week or two after mating, although some species wait several months. Many spiders lay several batches of eggs, usually at night when they are less likely to be seen by predators. There may be from one to over 1,000 eggs per batch. Most spiders lay their eggs on a circular pad of silk, and the female then covers them with more silk to form a protective cocoon known as the egg sac.

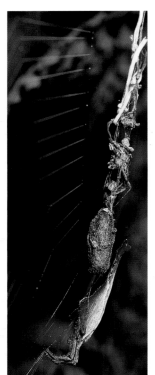

Ananse the Spider Man

In West Africa and the Caribbean, the hero of many folk tales is Ananse. He is both a spider and a man. When things are going well Ananse is a man, but in times of danger he becomes a spider. Ananse likes to trick the other animals and get the better of those who are much bigger than himself. He may be greedy and selfish, but he is also funny. He is a hero because he brought the gift of telling stories to people.

◄ **IN DISGUISE**
To hide their eggs from predators, spiders may camouflage the egg cases with plant material, insect bodies, mud or sand. This scorpion spider hangs her cocoon from a web like a string of rubbish, then poses as a dead leaf beneath them. Other species of spider hide their egg cases under stones or bark, or attach leaves around them like a purse.

▲ **SPINNING THE COCOON**
A *Nephila edulis* spider spins a cocoon. She uses special strong, loopy silk that traps a lot of air and helps to stop the eggs from drying out. Her eggs are covered with a sticky coating to attach them to the silk. The final protective blanket of yellow silk will turn green, camouflaging the cocoon.

◄ FLIMSY EGG CASE

The daddy-longlegs spider uses hardly any silk for her egg case. Just a few strands hold the eggs loosely together. Producing a large egg case uses up a lot of silk, so females with large egg cases often have shrunken bodies. The daddy-longlegs spider carries the eggs in her jaws, and so she cannot feed until the eggs have hatched.

SILK NEST ►

The woodlouse spider lays her eggs in a silken cell under the ground. She also lives in this shelter to hide from her enemies. At night, the spider emerges from its silken house to look for woodlice, which it kills with its enormous fangs.

◄ CAREFUL MOTHER

A green lynx spider protects her egg case on a cactus. She attaches the case with silk lines, like a tent's guy ropes, and attempts to drive off any enemies. If the predator persists, she cuts the silk lines and lets the cocoon swing in mid-air, balancing on top like a trapeze artist. If a female green lynx spider has to move her eggs to a safer place, she drags the case behind her with silk threads.

GUARD DUTY ►

Many female spiders carry their eggs around with them. This rusty wandering spider carries her egg case attached to her spinnerets (the organs at the back of the body that produce silk). Spiders that carry their eggs like this often sunbathe to warm them and so speed up their development.

Did you know? A female garden spider can lay over 1,000 eggs in under ten minutes.

Spiderlings

Most spider eggs hatch within a few days or weeks of being laid. The spiderlings (baby spiders) feed on egg yolk that is stored in their bodies, and they grow fast. Like insects, spiders molt to grow bigger. They shed their old skin and reveal a new, bigger skin that slowly hardens. Spiders molt several times. At first, spiderlings do not usually have any hairs, claws or color but after the first molt, the young spiders resemble tiny versions of their parents.

Most spiderlings look after themselves from the moment of hatching, but some mothers feed and guard their young until they leave the nest. Male spiders do not look after their young at all.

▲ **HATCHING**

These spiderlings are emerging from their egg case. They may have stayed inside the case for some time after hatching. Some spiders have an egg tooth to help break them out of the egg, but mother spiders may also help their young to hatch. Spiderlings from very different species look similar.

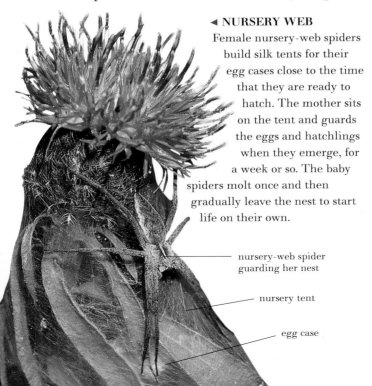

◄ **NURSERY WEB**

Female nursery-web spiders build silk tents for their egg cases close to the time that they are ready to hatch. The mother sits on the tent and guards the eggs and hatchlings when they emerge, for a week or so. The baby spiders molt once and then gradually leave the nest to start life on their own.

nursery-web spider guarding her nest

nursery tent

egg case

▲ **A SPIDER BALL**

Garden spiderlings stay together for several days after hatching. They form small gold and black balls that break apart if threatened by a predator, but re-form when the danger has passed.

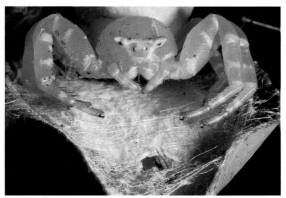

◄ BABY BODIES

A female crab spider watches over her young as they hatch. Spider eggs contain a lot of yolk, which provides a good supply of energy for the baby spiders. All spiderlings are well developed when they hatch, with the same body shape and number of legs as adults. Spiderlings, however, cannot produce silk or venom until after their first molt.

the spiderlings cling to special hairs on their mother's back for about a week

spotted wolf spider
(*Pardosa amentata*)

BABY CARRIER ►

Pardosa wolf spiders carry their egg cases around with them. When the eggs are ready to hatch, the mother tears open the case and the babies climb onto her back. If the spiderlings fall off, they can find their way back by following silk lines that the mother trails behind her.

silk threads

Did you know? When their mother dies, many young spiders eat her body.

▲ FOOD FROM MOM

The mothercare spider feeds her young on food brought up from her stomach, made of digested insects and the cells that line her gut. The babies shake her legs to beg for food. They grow faster than the young of species that have to feed themselves.

▲ BALLOON FLIGHT

Many spiderlings take to the air to find new places to live or to avoid being eaten by their brothers and sisters. On a warm day with light winds, they float through the air on strands of silk they have made. This is called ballooning.

Nesting Birds of Prey

Most bird species have a different mate every year, staying together only long enough to raise their young. However, birds of prey (also known as raptors) tend to stay with one mate for life. As with all birds, courting still takes place every year to help the pair strengthen their bond and to establish their hunting territory.

Within their territory, raptors build a nest in which the female lays her eggs. Birds of prey usually nest far apart from each other because they need a large hunting area. However, some species, such as griffon vultures and lesser kestrels, nest in colonies.

The nests and nesting sites vary greatly from species to species. Nests may be an elaborate structure of branches and twigs or no more than a simple bare patch of soil on a ledge. Many pairs of raptors return to the same nest every year, adding to it until it becomes a massive structure.

▲ FEED ME
This female hen harrier is brooding (sitting on her eggs). Like several other raptors, male hen harriers often catch prey for their mate while she is unable to hunt for herself. Hen harriers nest on the ground, and so they need to be well camouflaged. Both the birds and the nest are hard to spot.

Bonelli's eagle
(Hieraaetus fasciatus)

◄ SETTING UP HOME
A Bonelli's eagle repairs her clifftop perch, keeping a careful watch over her young chick. If there are no cliffs in her territory, the female builds her nest at the top of a tall tree. The nests measure up to 6 feet across and are used year after year. Scientists have ringed this chick's leg so that its movements can be traced throughout its life.

GO AWAY! ▶

By spreading his wings to make himself look bigger, a barn owl adopts a threatening pose to protect his nest. The female has already laid several eggs, which she will incubate (sit on to keep warm) for just over a month. During this time, the male feeds her, usually with rats, mice or voles, but sometimes with insects and small birds. If food is plentiful, the pair may raise two broods a year.

◀ IN A SCRAPE

This peregrine falcon has made a nest on a cliff ledge by simply clearing a small patch of ground. This type of nest is called a scrape. Many peregrines use traditional nesting sites, where birds have made their homes for centuries. Others have adapted to life in the city, making their scrapes on the ledges of skyscrapers, office buildings or churches.

◀ FULL UP

A secretary bird comes in to land on the huge treetop nest of a flock of weaver birds in search of its own nesting site. As the tree is full, the secretary bird will have to choose another site in which to nest. It prefers low thorny trees such as acacia. Its nest is made from sticks, lined with soft grass.

secretary bird
(*Sagittarius serpentarius*)

▲ SECOND-HAND NEST

A disused raven's nest has been adopted by this peregrine falcon. Peregrines often lay their eggs in nests abandoned by other birds. Female peregrines usually lay 3–4 eggs, and both parents take turns to incubate them. It takes about 30 days for the eggs to hatch.

Young Birds of Prey

Birds of prey chicks remain in the nest for different periods, depending on the species. The chicks of small raptors, such as merlins, are nest-bound for only about eight weeks, while the offspring of larger species, such as the golden eagle, stay in their nests for more than three months. Young vultures may stay for more than five months.

As raptor chicks grow, their thick down molts to reveal proper feathers. The chicks become stronger, and start to exercise their wings by standing up and flapping them. Eventually they are ready to make their first flight. This greatest step in the life of a young bird is called fledging. It takes weeks or even months before the young birds learn all of the flying and hunting skills they need to catch prey. Until then, they are still dependent on their parents for all their food.

▲ TAKING OFF
A young kestrel launches itself into the air. It is fully grown but still has juvenile plumage. Other adults recognize the plumage and do not drive the young bird away.

▼ GROWING UP
As a tawny owl grows, its appearance changes dramatically. At four weeks old, the chick is a fluffy ball of down. Three weeks later, it is quite well feathered. At three months, the young owl is fully feathered and can fly.

4 weeks old   7 weeks old   12 weeks old

adult pygmy falcon

juvenile pygmy falcon
(Poliohierax semitorquatus)

◀ BIG PYGMY

This pygmy falcon is still feeding its offspring, even though the chick is as big as its parent. In the early stages of the chick's life, the male pygmy falcon supplies all the food, while the female keeps the chick warm in the nest. Then both adults feed the fledgling, until the young bird learns to catch insects for itself. This skill can take up to two months to master.

▶ KESTREL COMPANY

A pair of month-old kestrels huddle together near their nest in an old farm building. They are fully feathered and almost ready to take their first flight. However, it will probably be another month before they learn to hunt.

◀ JUST PRACTICING

This young tawny owl is still unable to fly. It is flapping its wings up and down to exercise and strengthen the pectoral (chest) muscles that will enable it to fly. As the muscles get stronger, the young bird will sometimes lift off its perch. Eventually, often on a windy day, the owl will find itself flying in the air. On this first flight, it will not travel far, but within days, it will be flying as well as its parents.

tawny owl
(Strix aluco)

Crocodile Eggs

All crocodilians (crocodiles, alligators and gharials) lay eggs. The number of eggs laid by one female at a time ranges from about 10 to 90, depending on the species and the age of the mother. Older females lay more eggs. The length of time it takes for the eggs to hatch varies with the species and the temperature, and takes from 50 to 110 days. During this incubation period, bad weather can damage the babies developing inside the eggs. Too much rain may cause water to seep through the shells and drown the babies before they are born. Hot weather may make the inside of the egg overheat and harden the yolk, which means the baby cannot absorb the yolk and it starves to death. Another danger is that eggs laid by one female may be accidentally dug up and destroyed by another female digging a nest in the same place.

▲ **EGGS FOR SALE**
In many countries, people eat crocodilian eggs. They are harvested from nests and sold at local markets. This person is holding the eggs of a gharial. Each egg weighs about 4 ounces. The mother gharial lays about 40 eggs in a hole in the sand. She lays them in two tiers, separated from each other by a fairly thick layer of sand, and may spend several hours covering her nest.

▶ **NEST-SITTING**
The mugger crocodile of India digs a sandy pit about 10 inches deep in a river bank and lays between 10 and 50 eggs inside. She lays her eggs in layers and then covers them with a mound of twigs, leaves, soil and sand. During the 50–75 day incubation period, the female spends most of her time close to the nest. Female muggers are usually quite placid when they lay their eggs, and researchers have even been able to catch the eggs as they are laid.

▶ INSIDE VIEW

Curled tightly inside its egg, this alligator has its head and tail wrapped around its belly. Next to the developing baby is a supply of yolk, which provides it with food during incubation. Researchers have removed the top third of the shell to study the stages of growth. The baby will develop normally even though some of the shell is missing. As the eggs develop, they give off carbon dioxide gas. This reacts with moisture in the nest chamber and may make the shell thinner to let in more oxygen.

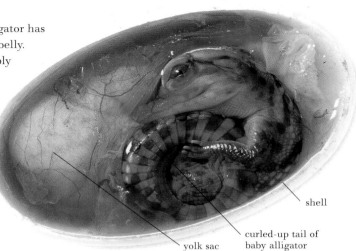

shell

curled-up tail of baby alligator

yolk sac

◀ CRACKING EGGS

A mother crocodile sometimes helps her eggs to hatch. When she hears the baby calling inside, she picks up the egg in her mouth. She rolls it to and fro against the roof of her mouth, pressing gently to crack the shell. The mother may have to do this for about 20 minutes before the baby breaks free from the egg.

EGGS IN THE NEST ▶

All crocodilian eggs are white and oval-shaped, with hard shells like a bird's eggs. This is the nest of a saltwater crocodile, and the eggs are twice the size of chickens' eggs. It takes a female saltwater crocodile about 15 minutes to lay between 20 and 90 eggs. The eggs take up to 90 days to hatch.

Crocodiles

Baby crocodilians make yelping, croaking and grunting noises from inside their eggs when it is time to hatch. The mother hears the noise and digs the eggs from the nest. The babies struggle free of their eggshells, sometimes with help from their mother. During this time, the mother is in a very aggressive mood and will attack any animal that comes near. Nile crocodile hatchlings are about 11 inches long, lively and very agile. They can give a human finger a painful nip with their sharp teeth. Their mother carries them gently in her mouth down to the water. She opens her jaws and waggles her head from side to side to wash the babies out of her mouth.

1 A female Nile crocodile has heard her babies calling from inside their eggs, so she knows it is time to help them escape from the nest. She scrapes away the soil and sand with her front feet and may use her teeth to cut through any roots that have grown between the eggs. Her help is very important as the soil has hardened during incubation. The hatchlings would find it difficult to dig their way up to the surface without her help.

the hatchling punches a hole in its hard shell with a forward-pointing egg tooth

2 This baby Nile crocodile has just broken through its eggshell. It used a horny tip on the snout, called the egg tooth, to break through. The egg tooth is the size of a grain of sand and disappears after about a week. The egg has become thinner during the long incubation, which makes it easier for the baby to break free.

Hatching

3 Struggling out of an egg is a long, exhausting process. When the hatchlings are half out of their eggs, they sometimes take a break so they can rest before completely leaving their shells. After all the babies have hatched, the mother crushes or swallows the rotten eggs that are left.

4 Even though they are fierce predators crocodilians make caring parents. The mother Nile crocodile lowers her head into the nest and delicately picks up the hatchlings and any unhatched eggs between her sharp teeth. She gulps them into her mouth. The weight of all the babies and eggs pushes down on her tongue to form a pouch that holds up to 20 eggs and live young. Male mugger crocodiles also carry the young like this and help hatchlings to escape from their eggs.

5 A young crocodilian's belly looks fat when it hatches. This is because it contains the remains of the yolk sac, which nourished it through the incubation period. The hatchling can swim and catch its own food right away, but it continues to feed on the yolk sac for up to two weeks. In Africa, baby Nile crocodiles usually hatch just before the rainy season. The wet weather brings an abundance of food, such as insects, tadpoles and frogs for the hatchlings. Baby crocodilians are very vulnerable to predators and are guarded by their mother for at least the first few weeks of life.

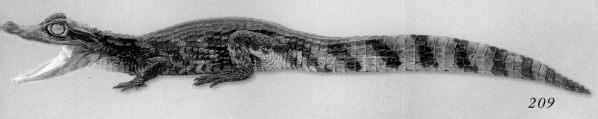

Young Crocodilians

Life is full of danger for juvenile (young) crocodilians. They are too small to defend themselves easily, despite their sharp teeth. All sorts of predators lurk in the water and on the shore, from birds of prey and pelicans, to monitor lizards, otters, tiger fish and even other crocodilians. Crocodilians lay many eggs, but not all of their young survive to hatch, and many that do, do not survive for long. Only one in ten alligators lives to the end of its first year. Juveniles often stay together in groups during the first weeks of life, yelping to each other if one gets separated. They also call loudly to the adults for help if they are in danger. By the time the juveniles are four years old, they stop making distress calls and start responding to the calls of other young individuals.

▲ INSECT DIET
A spiky-jawed Johnston's crocodile is about to snap up a dragonfly. Young crocodiles mainly eat insects. As they grow, they take larger prey, such as snails, shrimp, crabs and small fish. Their snouts gradually strengthen, so that they are able to catch bigger fish, which are the main food of this small Australian crocodile.

Did you know? 15 per cent of baby saltwater crocodiles do not survive a month.

◄ FAST FOOD
These juvenile alligators are in captivity and will grow twice as fast as they would in the wild. This is because they are fed at regular times and do not have to wait until they can catch a meal for themselves. It is also because they are kept in warm water—alligators stop feeding in cooler water. The best temperature for alligator growth is 85–90°F.

SMALL BUT SAFE ▶

Juveniles stay close to their mother for the first few weeks, resting on her back. No predator would dare to attack them there. Baby alligators are only about 10 inches long when they leave their eggs, but grow very quickly. When they have enough food to eat, male alligators grow about 12 inches a year until they are about ten years old.

▲ CROC CRECHE

A group of crocodilian young is called a pod. Here, a Nile crocodile guards her pod as they bask in the sun. At the first sign of danger, the mother rapidly vibrates her muscles and the young immediately dive underwater. A pod may stay in the same area for as long as two years.

▲ TOO MANY ENEMIES

The list of land predators that attack juvenile crocodilians includes big cats such as this leopard. Large wading birds, such as ground hornbills, marabou storks and herons, spear them with their sharp beaks in shallow water, while in deeper water, catfish, otters and turtles all enjoy a young crocodilian as a snack. Only about two per cent of all the eggs laid each year survive to hatch and grow into adults.

NOISY POD ▶

These crocodilians are caimans. A pod of juveniles, like this group, is a noisy bunch. By chirping and yelping for help, a juvenile warns its brothers and sisters that there is a predator nearby. The siblings quickly dive for shelter and hope that an adult will come to protect them. If a young Nile crocodile strays from its pod, it makes loud distress calls. Its mother, or any other female nearby, will pick up the youngster in her jaws and carry it back to the group.

Some species of snake give birth to live young, like mammals. Others lay eggs, like birds. Most egg-laying species abandon their eggs after laying them. However, some cobras and most pythons guard their eggs from predators and the weather.

Inside the egg, the baby snake feeds on the yolk. Once this has been used up the snake is fully developed and ready to hatch. All the eggs in a clutch tend to hatch at the same time.

1 As rat snakes develop inside the egg, they feed on the yolk. About eight weeks after being laid, the eggs begin to hatch.

Baby Snake Breakthrough

2 The baby snake is now fully developed and has become restless, twisting in its shell. It cannot get enough oxygen through the egg. The shell of a snake's egg is almost watertight, although water and gases, such as oxygen, pass in and out of it through tiny pores (holes). The baby snake cuts a slit in the shell with a sharp egg tooth on its snout. This egg tooth drops off a few hours after hatching.

3 After it has broken through the stretchy, leathery shell, the baby snake takes a rest. It pokes its nose through the slit in the egg to breathe the air and takes a first look at the strange and exciting world outside.

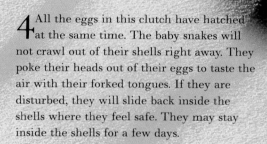

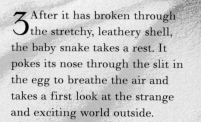

4 All the eggs in this clutch have hatched at the same time. The baby snakes will not crawl out of their shells right away. They poke their heads out of their eggs to taste the air with their forked tongues. If they are disturbed, they will slide back inside the shells where they feel safe. They may stay inside the shells for a few days.

Did you know? The mud snake lays over 100 eggs at a time.

5 Eventually, the baby snake slithers out of the egg. It may be as much as seven times longer than the egg because it was coiled up inside. It wriggles away to start a life on its own. It has to survive without any help from its parents.

rat snake
(*Ptyas mucosus*)

213

pope's
tree viper
(*Trimeresurus
popeorum*)

▲ TREE BIRTH
Tree snakes often give
birth in the branches of trees.
The membrane around each baby snake sticks
to the leaves and helps stop the baby from
falling out of the branches to the ground.

Snakes That Give Birth

Instead of laying eggs, some snakes
give birth to fully developed, live
young. Snakes that do this include
boas, rattlesnakes and adders. The
young develop in an egg inside the
mother's body. The surface of the
egg is a thin protective membrane
instead of a shell. The baby snake gets
its food from yolk inside the egg.
Anything from six to 50 babies are
born at a time, depending on the
species. The baby snakes are still inside
their membranes when they are born.

▲ BIRTH PLACE
The female sand viper chooses a quiet, remote
spot to give birth to her young. Snakes usually
give birth in a hidden place, where the young
are safe from enemies.

Did you know? An anaconda may have 100 babies at a time.

BABY BAGS ▶
These red-tailed boas
have just been born. They are
still inside their tough
membranes, which are made
of a thin, see-through material,
like the one inside the shell
of a hen's egg.

BREAKING FREE ▶

A baby rainbow boa has just pushed its head through the membrane that surrounds it. Snakes have to break free on their own. Each baby has an egg tooth to cut a slit in the membrane so that it can wriggle out. They usually do this a few seconds after birth.

◀ NEW BABY

A red-tailed boa has broken free of its membrane, the remains of which can be seen around the body. Some newborn snakes crawl off straight away, while others stay with their mother for a few days.

◀ COLOR CHANGE

Emerald tree boas are bright red when they are born. It takes a year for them to turn the vivid green of their parents.

Did you know? Baby boa constrictors grow from 20 inches to 40 inches in their first year.

emerald
tree boa
(*Epicrates
cenchria*)

Egg-laying Sharks

Sharks are fish, not mammals, and so their young do not suckle from their mother or need to breathe air. Sharks bring their young into the world in two ways. In most species, eggs grow into baby sharks inside the mother's body. The mother gives birth to active young called pups. In other species, the female shark lays eggs, each enclosed in a tough case or capsule. Young catsharks grow in cases like this. Each mating season, catsharks lay up to 20 cases and attach them to seaweed. A single pup develops inside each capsule. Catsharks do not guard or look after their egg cases in any way. Instead, they rely on the tough, leathery case to protect the pup inside.

▲ **EGG WITH A TWIST**
The egg case of a horn shark has a spiral-shaped ridge. The mother shark uses her mouth like a screwdriver to twist the case around and attach it firmly to gaps in rocks.

▲ **TIME TO LEAVE**
When it is ready to leave its egg, the baby horn shark uses special scales on its snout and fins to cut its way out of the tough egg case. The dorsal fins on its back have tough spines that protect it from the moment it emerges.

Mermaid's Purses
The mermaid is a mythical undersea creature with a woman's body and a fish's tail. In legends, mermaids lured men to their deaths with beautiful songs. Catshark egg cases, which are sometimes washed up on beaches, look like pouches, and are often called mermaid's purses.

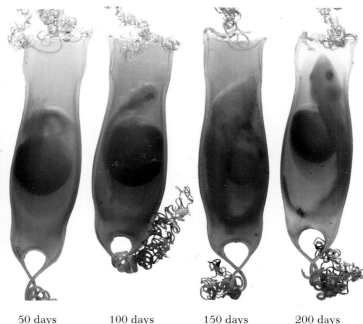

| 50 days | 100 days | 150 days | 200 days |

◄ ▲ IN THE SAC

In the earliest stages of development, the catshark pup is tiny, about the size of a pea. It is attached to a huge, yellow yolk sac from which it takes its food. Inside the egg case, the growing pup makes swimming movements, which keep the egg fluids and the supply of oxygen fresh. After nine months, the catshark pup breaks free of the case.

► SWELL SHARK

The length of time it takes the swell shark pup to grow and hatch from its case depends on the temperature of the sea water around it. In warm water, it can take just seven months. In cold water, it might take ten months. The pup has special skin teeth to tear its capsule open.

The Birth of a

A year after mating, pregnant lemon sharks arrive at Bimini Island, off the coast of Miami, in the Atlantic Ocean. Here, they give birth to their pups in a shallow lagoon where males do not enter. An adult male is quite likely to eat a smaller shark, even one of its own kind. In many species of shark, pregnant females leave the males and swim to safer nursery areas to give birth. Some scientists even believe that females lose their appetite at pupping time, to avoid eating their own young. After birth, the lemon shark pups live on their own.

1 By pumping sea water over her gills, a pregnant lemon shark can breathe while resting on the seabed. She gives birth on the sandy lagoon floor to the pups that have developed inside her for a year.

2 Baby lemon sharks are born tail first. Female sharks give birth to 5–17 pups at one time. Each pup is about 24 inches long. After her pups are born, a female lemon shark will not be able to mate again right away. Instead, she will rest for a year.

Lemon Shark Pup

3 A lemon shark gives birth to her pups in the shallows. The pups are still attached to the umbilical cord when born, but a sharp tug soon frees them. The small remora fish that follow the shark everywhere will feast on the discarded umbilical cord.

4 After birth, a baby lemon shark makes for safety in the shallow, muddy waters at the edge of the lagoon. It spends the first few years of its life among the tangled roots of the mangrove trees that grow there. The pup feeds on small fish, worms and shellfish. It must be wary of sharks larger than itself, which may try to eat it.

5 To avoid being eaten, young lemon sharks gather with others of the same size. Each group patrols its own section of the lagoon at Bimini. This young lemon shark is about one year old. When it is seven or eight, it will leave the safety of the lagoon and head for the open reefs outside.

The Birth

1 Some mares lie on their side during foaling, while others remain standing. The foal emerges head first, with its forelegs extended. It only takes a few minutes for it to be born. At first, it is still enclosed in the membrane in which it developed in the womb, but it soon breaks free by shaking itself or standing up.

2 The placenta, through which the foal received nutrients when it was still in the womb, comes out immediately after the birth. The mother might chew on this, but she does not eat it.

3 The mother licks the newborn foal all over to establish her bond with the baby. From now on, she will be able to recognize her foal from all others. It will take about a week, however, for the foal to know its mother.

Horses belong to the large group of animals called mammals. Like almost all mammals, the babies grow inside their mother, taking their nourishment from her rather than the yolk of an egg. This means the young can be born fairly well developed. All mammals feed their young on milk.

In the wild, horses, zebras and asses give birth when there is plenty of food and water around and weather is not too extreme. The breeding season is usually brief so that all the foals in one area will be born at about the same time. They have a greater chance of survival from predators if all of the foals are the same age, rather than being born in ones or twos throughout the year.

# of a Baby Horse

4 The newborn foal struggles to its feet. It will stand up within ten minutes of birth, and will soon be able to canter. The foal's first few days of life are taken up with feeding, practicing using its legs and napping. Feeds last for a few minutes each, and a rest may be between 20 minutes and one hour long.

5 The mother is very aggressive at this time. She chases other horses away and may even bite them. This ensures that the foal will imprint on her (recognize her as its source of food and protection) rather than any other animal in the herd. After about a week, the mare calms down, and the foal is allowed to meet with others of its own kind.

LOOKING FOR FOOD
Instinct tells this plains zebra foal that its mother's teats are found between the legs and the belly, but it might search between the forelegs before finding the right spot.

TWO YEARS UNTIL INDEPENDENCE
This wild ass foal will stay with its mother for two years. Asses usually foal every two years, but horses and zebras sometimes have one foal a year, if conditions are good.

Elephant Calves

Female elephants live in family groups with their mothers, sisters, daughters and their offspring. Like horses, females often have babies at about the same time, at the time of year that food is most plentiful.

An elephant's pregnancy lasts for nearly two years, and females only have one calf every four to six years. A female elephant may have her first calf at the age of 10 and her last when she is 50. She has between five and 12 babies in a lifetime.

Young elephant calves are highly vulnerable, and about a third do not survive to reach adulthood. Some are taken by predators, such as crocodiles, lions and tigers. Others drown or are crushed by falling trees. All the elephants in the group try to keep the calves safe.

▲ BIRTH TIME
A baby elephant emerges from its mother in a protective membrane called a birth sac. The other females in the group sniff the newcomer and softly touch it all over, while rumbling with excitement.

a baby elephant practices using its trunk

▲ TRUNK TRICKS
Baby elephants are curious and inquisitive. They want to touch and feel everything with their trunk. At first, they cannot control their long, wobbly nose. They trip over it or suck on it—just as human babies suck their thumbs. It takes them months of practice to learn how to use their trunks.

► THIRSTY CHILD
A calf sucks milk from its mother's breasts with its mouth. The milk is thin and watery, but very nourishing. Babies put on weight at a rate of 25–45 pounds per month.

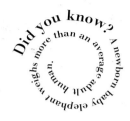

◄ LEARNING FAST

A young elephant has to master the technique of giving itself a dust bath. It must also learn to pick up and carry things with its trunk, drink, feed and have a mudbath. If a young elephant cannot reach water, the mother sucks up water in her trunk and squirts it down her baby's throat.

Did you know? A newborn baby elephant weighs more than an average adult human.

GUIDING TRUNK ►

At first, a baby elephant sticks close to its mother night and day. It is always within reach of a comforting touch from her strong, guiding trunk. The mother encourages her baby, helps it to keep up with other members of the herd and often pulls it back if it starts to stray. Baby elephants will die quickly if they are left on their own.

▲ PROPER FOOD

After a few months, calves begin to eat plants. A calf may put its trunk into its mother's mouth to taste her food and learn which plants are edible.

▲ HELPFUL RELATIVES

The survival of both mothers and calves depends greatly on the support of the family group. Each member of the group takes part in bringing up the babies. This helps the mother, and allows young female elephants to learn how to care for calves.

223

Caring Elephant Families

A baby elephant is brought up by its family in a fun-loving, easy-going and caring environment. At first, a calf spends a lot of time with its mother, but as it grows older and stronger, it begins to explore and make friends with other calves. Young elephants spend a lot of time playing together. They can do this because they feed on their mother's milk and so they do not have to spend all day finding food. Gradually, the calf learns all the skills it will need as an adult.

▲ BROTHERS AND SISTERS
A female elephant may have a calf every five years, but elephants do not become adults until they are about ten years old. Usually, just when the first calf can feed itself, another one arrives. The older calf still spends a lot of time with its mother.

Did you know? Female elephants become adult in nine or ten years but males mature a few years later.

◀ MOTHER'S MILK
A calf drinks its mother's milk until it is between four and six years old. By then, the mother usually needs her milk for the next baby. Even so, calves as old as eight have been known to push a younger brother or sister out of the way to steal a drink.

◄ PLAYTIME

A growing elephant learns a lot simply by playing. Male elephants push and shove each other to test their strength. Females play games with lots of chasing, like tag. Both males and females like to mess about in mud, dust and water.

▲ PROTECTING THE YOUNG

All the adults in a family are protective of the young. They shade calves from the sun and stand guard over them while they sleep. Small calves are vulnerable to attack from many other animals, including poisonous snakes.

Ganesh

In the Hindu religion of India, Ganesh is the elephant-headed god of wisdom and the remover of obstacles. Ganesh's father, the god Siva, is said to have cut off Ganesh's head. His mother, the goddess Parvati, was so angry that she forced Siva to give her son a new head. This new head turned out to be that of an elephant. Hindus seek good luck from Ganesh before the start of important business.

◄ LOTS OF MOTHERS

Allomothers are female elephants in the group that take a special interest in the upbringing of calves. They wake up the calf when it is time to travel, help it if it gets stuck in mud and protect it from danger.

225

Baby Great Apes

The great apes—gorillas, orangutans, chimpanzees, gibbons and bonobos—usually have one baby at a time and spend many years looking after their young, just as humans do. Most apes are pregnant for eight or nine months, although baby gibbons are born after seven or eight months.

Baby apes are much smaller than human babies and weigh only about half as much. This means that giving birth is easier for an ape than for a human mother. Both labor and birth are fairly swift and trouble-free. Newborn apes are almost helpless, but they have a very strong grip so they can cling to their mother's hair. She feeds them on her milk and may carry them around for four or five years as they gradually grow up and become more independent.

▲ **NEWBORN GORILLA**
This day-old gorilla is tiny and helpless as it clings to its mother's fur. Its wrinkled face is a pinkish color and its big ears stick out. Soon after birth, the baby's brown eyes open and peer curiously at its surroundings. Despite its long, skinny arms and legs, the baby gorilla is quite strong.

Did you know? A gorilla usually gives birth in less than an hour.

◄ **MILK FROM MOM**
A newborn baby gorilla depends on its mother's milk for nourishment. After six to eight months, it gradually begins to try different bits of plant food, but it continues to drink its mother's milk for at least two years.

chimpanzees
(Pan troglodytes)

gorillas
(Gorilla gorilla)

PIGGY-BACK ▶
Riding piggy-back on its mother's broad back, a baby gorilla watches the other gorillas and looks around its habitat as the group travels from place to place. This is the safest place for the young gorilla until it is strong enough to walk by itself.

▲ HITCHING A RIDE
Very young chimpanzees are carried underneath their mother, clinging on to her fur with their tiny fists. By the age of five to six months, a baby chimp starts to ride on its mother's back. It is alert, looking around and touching things.

◀ GOOD PARENTS
Baby gibbons depend on their mothers for warmth and milk. Gibbon fathers groom their babies and play with them. Siamang gibbon fathers look after their youngsters during the day.

▲ CHIMP CHILDHOOD
The bond between a mother chimpanzee and her baby is strong and lasts throughout their lives. A young chimp is completely dependent on its mother for the first five years. It stays close to its mother so that she can see and hear it.

227

The Life of a

MOTHER LOVE

There is a very strong bond between a mother orangutan and her baby. When she is not moving through the trees or feeding, the mother may groom her baby or suckle it, although she doesn't often play with it. A baby orangutan may scream and throw a tantrum to get its mother's attention.

Young orangutans live a different life from gorilla and chimpanzee babies. Instead of being brought up in a group, the orangutan's world is almost entirely filled by its mother. Most orangutans live alone, but following the birth of a baby, a mother becomes even more shy than usual. She tries to avoid other orangutans in order to protect her baby.

For the first year of its life, a baby orangutan is entirely dependent on its mother, and she cares for it without any help. A young orangutan stays with its mother for seven to nine years, gradually learning what to eat, where to find food, how to climb and swing through the trees safely, and how to make a nest to sleep in.

MOTHER'S MILK

For the first year of its life, a baby orangutan drinks its mother's milk and clings to her chest or back. After a year, it starts to eat solid food but it continues to suck for another three to five years. Like most baby mammals, orangutans are keen to take their mother's milk for as long as possible.

Young Orangutan

NEST-BUILDING
Orangutans sleep in nests made with leafy branches. During their second year, young orangutans experiment with making their own nests.

PLAYTIME
Although they are usually solitary, on the rare occasions young orangutans meet they wrestle and play together in the forest. They may get so carried away that they do not notice when their mother leaves. Then they have to hurry after her, screaming angrily as they go.

SOLID FOOD
To start her baby on solid food, a mother orangutan partly chews up bits of food and then presses them into the baby's mouth. Young orangutans eagerly take the solid food.

A NEW BABY
When an orangutan is between five and eight years old, its mother may give birth again. The new baby takes most of the mother's attention, and the young orangutan becomes more independent. Even so, it may stay with its mother for a year or more after the new baby is born.

229

Great Ape Childhood

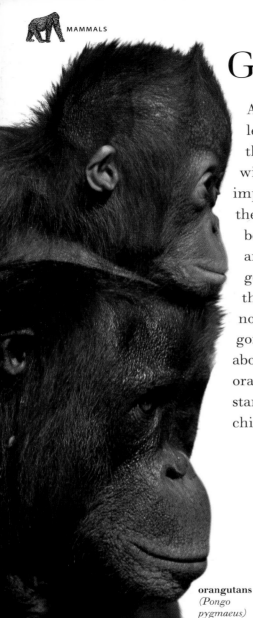

Apes spend a long time growing up. As well as learning how to move, feed and defend themselves, they have to know how to behave with others of their own kind. This is especially important for chimpanzees and gorillas because they live in large groups. Young apes do not become independent of their mothers until they are aged about eight. Female orangutans and gorillas will not have babies of their own until they are about ten years old, and female chimps not until they are 14. Male orangutans and gorillas will not have offspring until they are about 15 years of age. When they are grown up, orangutans and gibbons leave their parents to start a life of their own. Most gorillas and female chimps also leave the group they were born into.

orangutans
(*Pongo pygmaeus*)

▲ **MOTHER AND BABY**
Female orangutans spend most of their adult lives caring for their offspring. An orangutan may have only four young in her lifetime.

▲ **APE EXPLORER**
Young chimps love to explore, moving farther away from their mothers as they test their climbing skills. At the first sign of danger, though, they run back to their mothers.

230

▲ SPEEDY GORILLAS

Baby gorillas develop through the same stages of movement as human babies, only much faster. They can crawl at nine weeks of age and walk by nine months—an age when most human babies have only just started to crawl.

◄ PLAYING THE GAME

Little chimps have a lot of free time, which they spend at play. Young females spend much of their time playing with the babies in their group. Through playing, the chimps learn the rules of chimpanzee society.

chimpanzee
(Pan troglodytes)

Did you know?
Young gorillas have a white tuft on their rear to help their mothers find them.

▲ FOOD FROM MOTHER

A chimpanzee watches its mother and other chimps to find out what is good to eat. Young chimps chew the other end of whatever food their mother is eating.

AT PLAY ►

Young gorillas wrestle, chase, playfight and climb and slide all over the adults. This helps them to test their strength, build up their muscles and learn how to get along with other gorillas.

Inside a Bear Den

Bear cubs are born naked and helpless at the harshest time of year. They are absolutely tiny compared to the size of an adult bear and need to be protected from the cold weather as well as from predators. A den, hidden away from the outside world, makes a perfect home. The den can be in a cave, a hollow tree or a self-made hollow.

The female bear does not leave the den for the first few months. She does not hunt, but relies on her fat reserves to survive. Producing enough milk to nourish her cubs takes a lot of energy, and a mother bear is only able to feed them if she has eaten enough food in the months before.

▲ **BLIND AND HELPLESS**
Ten-day-old brown bear cubs nestle into their mother's fur for warmth. With their eyes and ears tightly closed shut, they are totally dependent on her. The cubs remain in the den until May or June when they are about four months old.

Did you know? Polar bear cubs are no bigger than guinea pigs when they are born.

◄ **POLAR TWINS**
A polar bear mother tends her two young. The family leaves its den between late February and April depending on where it lives. The farther north the bears are, the later in the year they emerge.

polar bear
(Ursus maritimus)

▲ TRIPLE TROUBLE

This American black bear has given birth to three healthy cubs. Females may have up to four cubs at one time. Newborn black bear cubs are about the size of a rat, but they grow quickly. They leave the den in April or May.

▲ PANDA BABY

At Wolong breeding station in Sichuan, China, a baby giant panda is put in a box to be weighed. Giant pandas give birth to one or two cubs in a cave or tree hollow. If twins are born, the mother often rears only one, leaving the other to die.

◄ MOTHER'S MILK

Three-month-old polar bear cubs feed on their mother's milk. Unlike most bear cubs, polar bears are born covered with fine hair to help keep them warm in the bitter Arctic weather.

IN THE DEN ►

Newborn American black bears weigh less than 12 ounces, which is about the same as a can of soda pop. Their small size and lack of fur makes them vulnerable to the cold. The mother cleans and dries the cubs, then cuddles them close. The den is lined with branches, leaves, and grasses to make a warm blanket. The mother spends a lot of time grooming her cubs and keeps the den scrupulously clean by eating their droppings.

Snow Dens

From late October, a pregnant female polar bear digs a snow den. Usually it is some distance from the sea, on a slope facing south. This means the den's entrance and exit hole faces towards the sun, which is low on the horizon in early spring. The sun's rays help to warm the den.

The mother bear gives birth during the harshest part of winter, when permanent night covers the Arctic. The den is kept warm and snug with heat from her body. A tunnel to the nursery chamber slopes upwards so that warm air rises and collects in the chamber, which can be 40°F warmer than outside.

1 A bank of snow makes an ideal site for a polar bear's winter den. The pregnant female bear digs about 15 feet into the south side of the snowdrift. The wind in the Arctic blows mainly from the north, so the snow piles up on the other side.

2 This picture is an artist's impression of the inside of a polar bear's den. The cubs are about three months old and they are almost ready to leave their snow home for the first time. Polar bear cubs are born between late November and early January, but don't leave the den until the spring.

3 The female polar bear emerges from her winter home. She drives two holes through the walls of the den and helps the cubs make their first journey outside. The family remains near the den site for a few days so the cubs become used to the cold.

234

for Polar Bears

4 Sitting upright in a snow hollow, a female polar bear nurses her cubs. She differs from other female bears in that she has four working nipples rather than six. Her cubs stay with her for three years, which is a year longer than the average for bears. During the years they spend with her, the cubs will learn how to survive in the cold Arctic conditions and also how to hunt seals for food.

5 The cubs play outside in the snow during the short days, and shelter in the den at night and during storms. Soon the family leaves the den altogether and heads towards the sea where the mother can hunt and feed.

6 The cubs' first journey is often a long one. They may have to walk up to 14 miles to reach the sea ice where they will see their first seal hunt. The mother takes great care to avoid danger on the journey. She looks out for adult male polar bears who might try to kill her cubs.

235

Bear Cubs

Young bears spend their first 18 months to three years with their mother. If she dies, they may be adopted by another mother with cubs the same age. The cubs learn everything from their mother. She teaches them how to recognize the best food and where and when to find it. The cubs must also learn how to escape danger and how to find a winter den or shelter in a storm. Without this schooling, the young bears would not survive. Mothers and cubs communicate by calling, particularly if they become separated from each other.

During their development, cubs must keep out of the way of large male bears who might attack and kill them.

▲ SAFE IN THE BRANCHES
Black bear cubs instinctively know that they should head for the nearest tree when danger threatens. It is easier for a mother to defend a single tree than a scattered family.

▼ FEEDING TIME
A mother brown bear suckles her twins. Her milk is thick and rich in fats and proteins, but low in sugars. It has three times the energy content of human or cow milk. The milk also contains antibodies, which help protect the cubs from disease.

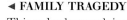

brown bear
(Ursus arctos)

◀ LEAVING THE FAMILY

Young bears on their own, such as this brown bear, often become thin and scrawny. Despite being taught by their mothers where and how to feed, they are not always successful. At popular feeding sites, such as fishing points, they may be chased off by larger bears. When the time comes for young bears to look after themselves, the mother either chases them away or is simply not there when they return to look for her.

A LONG APPRENTICESHIP ▶

Polar bear cubs are cared for by their mother for much longer than other bear cubs. They need to master the many different hunting strategies used by their mother to catch seals. These are not something that the cubs know instinctively, but skills that they must learn.

polar bear
(Ursus maritimus)

Did you know? Giant panda cubs are the first bears to leave their mother at 18 months old.

◀ FAMILY TRAGEDY

This polar bear cub is the victim in a tragic tug-of-war. A male bear has attacked the cub and its mother is trying to save it. Female bears fight ferociously to protect their young, but are often unsuccessful against the larger males. About 70 per cent of polar bear cubs do not live to their first birthday. Attacks by adult male bears, starvation, disease and the cold are the usual causes of death.

Big Cat Babies

The cubs (babies) of a big cat are usually born with spotted fur and closed eyes. They are completely helpless. The mother cat looks after them on her own with no help from the father. She gives birth in a safe place called a den. For the first few days after birth, she stays very close to her cubs so that they can feed on her milk. She keeps them warm and cleans the cubs by licking them all over. The cubs grow quickly. They can crawl even before their eyes open, and they soon learn to hiss to defend themselves.

▲ SNOW CUB

Snow leopard cubs have white fur with dark spots, and they are always born in the spring. The cubs begin to follow their mothers around when they are about three months old. By winter, they will be almost grown up.

MOTHERLY LOVE ▶

Tiger cubs are capable killers by the time they are 11 months old. They stay with their mothers, however, until they are two or even three years of age. A female tiger does all she can to protect her young, but often at least half of the litter dies. Predators may kill the cubs, or sometimes they starve to death if the mother cannot catch enough food.

cheetah cub
(*Acinonyx jubatus*)

IN DISGUISE ▶
A cheetah cub is covered in long, woolly fur. This makes it resemble the African honey badger, a very fierce animal, which may help to discourage predators. The mother cheetah does not raise her cubs in a den, but moves them around every few days.

▲ BRINGING UP BABY
Female pumas give birth to up to six kittens at a time. The mother has several pairs of teats for the kittens to suckle from. Each baby has its own teat and will use no other. They will take their mother's milk for at least three months, and from about six weeks they will also eat meat.

▲ ON GUARD
Two lionesses guard the entrance to their den. Lions are social cats and share the responsibility of keeping guard. Dens are kept very clean so that there are no smells to attract predators.

▲ MOVING TO SAFETY
If at any time a mother cat thinks her cubs are in danger, she will move them to a new den. She carries the cubs one by one, gently grasping the loose skin at their necks between her teeth.

239

Cubs Growing Up

Young cubs have to learn all about life as an adult big cat so that they can eventually look after themselves. Their mother teaches them as much as she can, and the rest they learn through play. As cubs play, they learn how to judge distances and when to strike to kill prey quickly, without getting injured or killed themselves. The exact games cubs play vary from one species of cat to another, because each has different hunting techniques to learn. Cheetahs, for instance, playfight using their paws to knock each other over. Lions play by biting each other's throats.

Mothers and cubs generally use very high-pitched sounds to communicate, but if the mother senses danger, she growls at her cubs to tell them to hide.

▲ **PRACTICE MAKES PERFECT**
These cheetah cubs are learning to kill a Thomson's gazelle. When the cubs are about 12 weeks old, a mother cheetah brings back live injured prey for them to kill. They instinctively know how to do so, but need practice to get it right.

▼ **FOLLOW MY LEADER**
Curious cheetah cubs watch an object intently, safe beside their mother. At about six weeks, the cubs start to go on hunting trips with her. They are able to keep up by following her white-tipped tail through the tall grass.

cheetah
(*Acinonyx jubatus*)

THE CLASSROOM ▶

These lion cubs lounge on a fallen tree. From here they watch the adults hunt, as if in a big, open-air classroom. Females stay in the same pride (group) all their lives, but young males will leave at about three years old.

lion cubs
(Panthera leo)

◀ WHAT IS IT?

Three young lions sniff at the shell of a tortoise. Cubs learn to be cautious when dealing with unfamiliar objects. First, the object is tapped with a paw, before being explored further with the nose. Cubs' milk teeth are replaced with permanent canine teeth at about two years old. Not until then can they begin to hunt and kill big animals.

TAIL TOY ▶

A mother leopard's tail is a good thing for her cub to learn to pounce on. She twitches it so that the cub can develop accurate timing and coordination. As the cub grows, it practices on rodents and then bigger animals until it can hunt for itself. Once they leave their mothers, female cubs usually establish a territory close by, while males go farther away.

241

Newborn Wolves

Most wolf packs have between 8 and 24 members. Only the leaders will mate and have cubs, but every pack member then helps to bring up the cubs.

Newborn wolves are helpless. They cannot hear, their eyes are tightly closed and their legs are too weak to allow them to stand. The cubs squirm around and huddle close to their mother for warmth. Like all mammals, their first food is their mother's rich milk.

After one or two weeks, the cubs' eyes open and they begin to take notice of their surroundings. They take their first wobbly steps and scramble over each other in the den. At about five weeks, the cubs start to take solid food as well as milk. Half-chewed meat, stored in the stomach of an adult wolf, is brought to the den and regurgitated (coughed up) when the cubs beg for food.

▲ AT THE DEN

Wolf cubs take a first look at the big world outside their den. For nearly eight weeks, their only experience has been the burrow—a 13-foot-long tunnel dug in soft earth with room for an adult wolf to creep along. The cubs sleep in a cozy chamber at the end.

Did you know? The mother of the wolf cubs sleeps in a hollow near the entrance of the den.

NURSING MOTHER ►

Like bears, most wolves are born in a den, and the female stays with her cubs for the first few weeks. A wolf mother, however, does not have to rely on fat reserves as bears do. Her mate, and the rest of the pack, bring food so that she does not have to go hunting. She needs large quantities of food to produce enough milk for her cubs.

▼ CUBS IN DANGER

These wolf cubs are six or seven weeks old. Not all cubs are born in a den. Some are born in a sheltered hollow, or in a nest flattened in long grass. There are many dangers for cubs in the open, including being snatched by predators such as bears and eagles. Many do not survive to adulthood.

gray wolf cubs
(Canis lupus)

Romulus and Remus

According to ancient Roman legend, Romulus and Remus were twin brothers who were abandoned as babies on a remote hillside. A she-wolf found them and brought them up, feeding them on her milk. Both brothers survived, and Romulus went on to found the city of Rome.

▲ HUNGRY PUPPIES

An African hunting dog suckles her pups. They suck milk from two sets of nipples on her underside. Female hunting dogs often have more nipples than other canids, because they have the biggest litters and therefore the most mouths to feed. As the pups' sharp teeth begin to hurt, she will wean them onto meat.

▲ RARE CUBS

In the mountains of Ethiopia, a female Simien wolf guards her litter of five cubs. Simien wolves are much rarer than other wolves. These cubs look healthy, so have a good chance of surviving long enough to breed as adults.

243

Older Wolf Cubs

At eight weeks old, wolf cubs are very lively. Their snouts have grown longer, their ears stand up and they look much more like adult wolves. They bound about on long, strong legs. Now weaned off milk, they live on a diet of meat brought by the adults. As they leave the safety of the den, the other pack members gather round and take great interest in the cubs. The cubs' new playground is the rendezvous, the safe place at the heart of wolf-pack territory where the adults gather. This is usually a sheltered, grassy spot near a stream where the cubs can drink. Here they develop their hunting skills by pouncing on mice and insects. As they playfight, they establish a ranking order that mirrors the social order in the pack.

▲ CARRIED AWAY

A wolf carries a cub to safety by seizing the loose skin at the scruff of its neck in its teeth. This adult is most likely the cub's mother or father, but it may be another member of the pack. All the adult wolves are very tolerant of the youngsters to begin with. Later, as the cubs grow up, they may be punished with a well-placed nip if they are naughty.

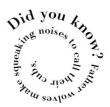

Did you know? Father wolves make squeaking noises to call their cubs.

SHARING A MEAL ▶

A young African hunting dog begs for food by whining, wagging its tail and licking the adult's mouth. The adult responds by arching its back and regurgitating a meal of half-digested meat from its stomach. The pups grow quickly on this diet. At the age of four months, they are strong enough to keep up with the pack when it goes hunting.

▼ PRACTICE MAKES PERFECT

Two Arctic fox cubs practice their hunting skills by pouncing on one another. Young cubs playfight to establish a ranking order. By the age of 12 weeks, one cub has managed to dominate the others. He or she may go on to become leader of a new pack.

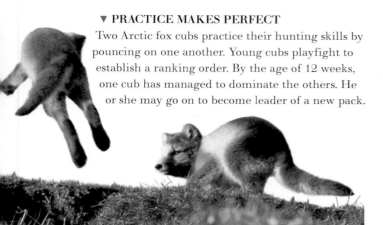

Wolfchild

Rudyard Kipling's Jungle Book, *which was published in 1894, is set in India. The book tells the story of Mowgli, a young boy who is abandoned and brought up by wolves in the jungle. When Mowgli becomes a man he fights his archenemy, the tiger Shere Khan. Kipling's tale was inspired by many true-life accounts of wolf-children who grew up in the wild in India during the 1800s.*

▲ YOUTHFUL CURIOSITY

Young maned wolves investigate their surroundings. Females usually bear three cubs at most. Newborn young have gray-brown fur, short legs and snouts. Later they develop long legs and handsome red fur.

ALMOST GROWN ▶

These two young wolves are almost full grown. Cubs can feed themselves at about ten months, but remain with the pack to learn hunting skills. At about two or three years old, many are turned out. They wander alone or with brothers or sisters until they find mates and start new packs.

Baby Whales

BIRTH DAY
A bottlenose dolphin gives birth. The baby is born tail-first. This birth is taking place near the bottom of an aquarium. In the wild, birth takes place close to the surface so the baby can surface quickly and start breathing.

Although they live in the sea, whales are mammals, which means that they breathe air and the mother feeds her young with milk. Many whales are enormous, and so are their babies. A newborn blue whale can weigh up to 2½ tons, which is twice as much as a family car.

The first thing a newborn whale must do is to take a breath. Its mother and perhaps another whale may help it up to the surface. After that, the calf can breathe and swim unaided. Baby whales feed on their mother's milk for several months until they learn to take solid food such as fish. Mother and calf may spend most of the time alone, or join nursery schools with other mothers and calves.

SUCKLING
A beluga mother suckles her young. Her fatty milk is very nutritious, and the calf grows rapidly. It will drink milk for up to two years. At birth the calf's body is dark grey, but it slowly lightens as the calf matures.

and Dolphins

AT PLAY

A young
Atlantic spotted
dolphin and its
mother play together,
twisting, turning,
rolling and touching
each other with their
flippers. During play,
the young dolphin learns
the skills it will need later
in life when it has to fend for
itself. The youngster is darker
than its mother and has no spots.
These do not start to appear until
it is about a year old.

Did you know? Blue whales are born in tropical waters, but nine months later they are thousands of miles away in cold polar waters.

TOGETHERNESS

A humpback whale calf sticks closely to its mother as she swims slowly in Hawaiian waters. The slipstream (water flow, created by the mother's motion) helps pull it along. For the first few months of its life, the calf will not stray far from its mother's side.

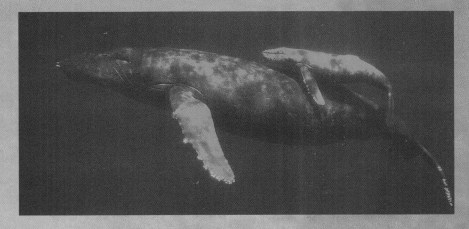

Glossary

abdomen
The central section of an animal's body that holds the reproductive organs and part of the animal's digestive system.

adapt
To change in order to survive in changed conditions. It usually takes place over many generations in a process called evolution.

alarm
Sudden fear that is produced by an awareness of danger.

ambush
To hide and wait, and then make a surprise attack.

antennae (singular: antenna)
The 'feelers' on top of an insect's head, which are used for smelling, touching and tasting.

arthropod
An animal without a backbone that has many jointed legs and an exoskeleton on the outside of its body. Arthropods include spiders, insects, crabs and woodlice.

bird of prey
A bird, such as an eagle, that catches and kills its prey with powerful hooked claws called talons.

body language
The communication of information by means of conscious or sometimes unconscious bodily gestures and facial expressions.

bonding
To form strong emotional attachments, especially between a mother and her baby.

brackish
Water that is not fresh and is slightly salty.

bray
A loud cry that asses and zebras make, sounding like a loud laugh.

broad-leaved
Trees with broad, flat leaves. The term is often used to distinguish these trees from conifers.

brood
(1) The number of babies a mother has at one time.
(2) When a bird sits on its eggs to incubate them.

burrow
A hole in the ground, usually dug by a small animal for shelter or defence.

camouflage
The colours or patterns on an animal's body that allow it to blend in with its surroundings.

carnivore
An animal that feeds on the flesh of other animals.

carrion
The remains of a dead animal.

caterpillar
The second, larval stage in the life of a butterfly or moth, after it has hatched from the egg. A caterpillar has a long tube-like body with 13 segments and many legs. It has no wings.

chrysalis
The third, pupal stage in the lives of butterflies and moths, during which the caterpillars are transformed into adults. Moth chrysalises are often enclosed in silken cocoons.

clutch
The number of eggs laid by a female at one time.

cocoon
(1) The shelter spun from silk thread by some insect larvae in which they turn into pupae.
(2) A silky covering or egg case made to protect a spider's eggs.

cold-blooded
An animal whose temperature varies according to its surroundings.

colony
A group of the same species of animal or plant that live close together.

conflict
A disagreement or fight between two or more animals.

congregate
To gather in a crowd.

coniferous
Trees that bear their seeds in cones. They have needle-like leaves and usually grow in cool or cold areas. Most are evergreens.

courtship
The process of attracting and establishing a bond with a mating partner.

crocodilian
A member of the group of animals that includes crocodiles, alligators, gharials and caimans.

cultivated
Land or soil that is especially prepared and used for growing crops.

deciduous
Trees that drop their leaves for part of the year. They grow in cool, temperate areas.

diet
The range of food an animal eats.

digestion
The process by which food is broken down so that it can be absorbed into the body.

domestic
Animals that do not live in the wild but are kept as a pet or farm animal.

dominance
A system between animals, such as lions, in which one or a few animals rule the group and have first choice over the other, more junior members.

down
Fine, hairy feathers for warmth not flight. Young chicks have only down and no flight feathers.

dragline
The line of silk on which a spider drops down, often to escape danger, and then climbs back up.

drought
A prolonged amount of time without any rainfall.

egg tooth
A small tooth that snakes and birds use to help them escape from the egg when they hatch.

environment
The conditions of an area an animal lives in.

equid
Horses and horse-like animals, such as asses and zebras.

evolution
The natural change of living organisms over very long periods of time, so that they become better suited to the conditions they live in.

expression
A look on an animal's face that shows how it is feeling.

feral
Domestic animals that have escaped or been abandoned and are now living freely in the wild.

fertilization
The joining together of a male sperm and a female egg to start a new life.

fledging/fledgling
The time when a bird starts to fly is called fledging. A fledgling is a young bird that has just reached this stage.

grassland
Open areas covered in grass.

grazer
An animal that feeds on grass, e.g. horses, antelopes.

groom
The way an animal cares for its coat and skin. It can be carried out by the animal itself or by one animal for another.

habitat
The particular place where a group of plants or animals live.

harem
A collection of female animals overseen by a single male.

herbivores
Animals that only eat plant food.

herd
A group of animals that remain together. Elephant herds are made up of several family units, together with adult bulls. A large herd may have 1,000 individual elephants.

hibernation
A time when body processes slow down and an animal sleeps during the cold, winter months.

incisor teeth
Sharp teeth in the front of a mammal's mouth that are used for biting and nibbling food.

incubation
Keeping eggs warm so that development can take place.

infrasounds
Sounds that have a frequency below the range of human hearing. They are made by crocodiles and other aquatic animals and can travel long distances through water.

insect
An invertebrate (lacking a backbone) animal that has three body parts, six legs and usually two pairs of wings. Ants, bees and butterflies are all insects.

instinct
A behaviour that an animal can carry out from a very early stage without having to learn how to do it. All members of a species have the same instincts.

intestine
Part of an animal's gut where food is broken down and absorbed into the body.

juvenile
A young animal. In birds, juveniles have not grown their adult plumage.

krill
Tiny crustaceans that are the main food for many of the baleen whales.

labour
The process of giving birth.

lagoon
A shallow, sheltered part of the sea, close to land.

larva (plural: larvae)
The young of insects that undergo complete metamorphosis, such as beetles and butterflies. Larvae are also called grubs, caterpillars or maggots.

Latin name
The scientific name for a species.

life cycle
The series of stages in the life of an animal as it grows up and becomes an adult.

litter
The number of babies a mother gives birth to at one time.

mammal
A warm-blooded animal with a backbone. Mammals breathe air and feed their offspring on milk from the mother's body. Most have hair or fur. Whales and dolphins are mammals, although they live in the sea.

mandibles
The jaw-like mouthparts that are present in some insects.

mantling
The behaviour of birds of prey where they spread their wings to conceal a catch. This is to prevent other hungry birds from stealing their kill.

mare
Adult female horse.

marsh
An area of land that is very wet for most of the year.

matriarch
The female head of a group, e.g. a queen bee.

mature
Developed enough to be capable of reproduction.

metamorphosis
The transformation of a young insect into an adult. Beetles and butterflies have four stages in their life cycle: egg, larva, pupa and adult. This is called complete metamorphosis.

migration
When animals, usually birds, travel (or migrate) regularly from one habitat to another because of changes in the weather or their food supply, or in order to breed.

milk teeth
The teeth of a young mammal that are replaced by adult teeth later.

mobbing
When prey birds gang up against their predators and try to drive them away.

moulting
(1) When a young, growing insect, spider or snake sheds its skin and grows a new, larger one.
(2) When a bird loses its feathers and grows new ones.

nectar
The sweet juice made by flowers that is the main food for adult butterflies and moths and many other insects.

nectary
A specialized gland in flowering plants that produces nectar.

nocturnal
Animals that are active at night.

nutrients
The goodness in foods that is essential for life.

pack
A collection of animals that live and feed together in a group, e.g. wild dogs.

palps
Short stalks that project from the mouthparts of a butterfly, moth or spider which act as sensors. They play an important part in finding food and food plants.

parasites
Animals that live on other animals and harm them by feeding on them, although they do not usually kill them. Fleas and ticks are parasites.

pecking order
A social hierarchy that exists among some animal groups.

pesticides
Chemicals that are sprayed on to plants to kill pests, especially insects.

pheromone
A chemical scent released by animals to attract members of the opposite sex and in some cases to attack prey.

photosynthesis
The process whereby green plants manufacture carbohydrates from carbon dioxide and water, using the light energy from the sun.

piracy
When a bird of prey makes a killing and is then intimidated by another bird into dropping its kill.

placenta
The end of the umbilical cord, attached to the womb, through which an unborn mammal receives nutrients from its mother.

plain
An area of flat land without any hills.

playfight
The games that young animals play to sharpen fighting skills that will be used in later life.

plumage
The covering of feathers on a bird's body.

pod
A group of animals. In crocodilians, this refers to newly hatched animals. In whales and dolphins, a pod is a group which hunt together.

posture
The way that an animal holds its body whilst standing, sitting or walking. Posture can show others that they are strong and dominant.

predator
An animal that hunts and kills other animals for food.

prehensile
A part of an animal that is adapted for grasping, e.g. a giraffe's lips.

prey
An animal that is hunted by other animals for food.

pride
The name for a group of lions.

primate
A group of mammals that includes monkeys, apes and humans. They all have flexible fingers and toes and forward facing eyes.

proboscis
The long, tongue-like mouthparts of certain insects, such as the butterfly, which act like drinking straws to suck up liquid.

prosimian
The group of primates that includes lemurs, lorises, pottos and tarsiers. Prosimians have smaller brains than other primates.

pupa (plural: pupae)
The third stage in the life of many insects, between the larval stage and the adult.

rainforest
A tropical forest where it is hot and wet all year round.

raptor
Any bird of prey. From the Latin word *rapere* meaning to seize, grasp or take by force.

regurgitate
To bring up food that has already been swallowed.

reptile
A scaly, cold-blooded animal with a backbone, including tortoises, turtles, snakes, lizards and crocodilians.

ritual
A procedure or actions that are repeated regularly.

ruminant
An even-toed, hoofed mammal, such as a cow, which eats and later regurgitates its food to eat again to extract as much nourishment as possible.

salt gland
An organ on a crocodile's tongue that gets rid of excess salt.

savanna
A large area of grassland in a hot region, particularly found in Africa. Savannas may have scattered trees and bushes but there is not enough rain for forests to grow.

scavenger
An animal that feeds on the remains of dead animals.

scent
A smell. For instance, social insects give off scents to give a wide range of messages that influence the behaviour within the nest.

scrape
A patch of ground cleared by a bird to lay its eggs on.

scrub
A harsh, dry area of land dominated by low-growing bushes.

semi-wild
Domestic animals that are left to run free over a large area of land for most of the year.

signal
A message in the form of sound or a gesture. A wolf's howl will gather a pack together for a hunt.

sociable animal
An animal that prefers to be in the company of other animals rather than being alone, e.g. lions.

social animal
An animal that lives in a group with other animals of its own kind. They co-operate with other group members e.g. horses and elephants.

solitary
Animals that prefer to live alone and without companions, e.g. snakes.

species
A group of animals that share similar characteristics and can breed together to produce fertile young.

talons
A hooked claw, especially on a bird of prey.

temperate
Areas of the Earth that have a moderate climate. They are not as hot as the tropics nor as cold as the Arctic and the Antarctic.

termite
An ant-like social insect that lives in highly organized colonies, mainly in tropical areas.

territory
An area that an animal uses for feeding or breeding. Animals defend their territories against others of the same species.

tundra
The cold, treeless land in far northern regions of the world, which is covered with snow for much of the year.

umbilical cord
The cord running between an unborn baby mammal and its mother, through which it receives nutrients.

warm-blooded
An animal that maintains its body temperature at the same level all the time.

warning colours
Bright colours that show others that an animal is poisonous. Bright colours also warn predators to keep away.

womb
An organ in the body of female mammals in which young grow and are nourished until birth.

yolk
Food material that is rich in protein and fats. It nourishes a developing embryo inside an egg.

Index

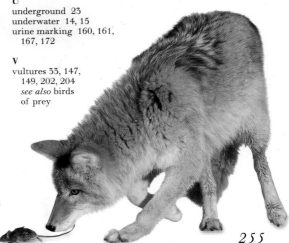

This edition is published by Lorenz Books

Lorenz Books is an imprint of Anness Publishing Ltd
Hermes House, 88–89 Blackfriars Road, London SE1 8HA
tel. 020 7401 2077; fax 020 7633 9499
www.lorenzbooks.com; info@anness.com

© Anness Publishing Ltd 2002, 2004

UK agent: The Manning Partnership Ltd, 6 The Old Dairy, Melcombe Road, Bath BA2 3LR;
tel. 01225 478444; fax 01225 478440; sales@manning-partnership.co.uk

UK distributor: Grantham Book Services Ltd, Isaac Newton Way, Alma Park Industrial Estate, Grantham, Lincs NG31 9SD;
tel. 01476 541080; fax 01476 541061; orders@gbs.tbs-ltd.co.uk

North American agent/distributor: National Book Network, 4501 Forbes Boulevard, Suite 200, Lanham, MD 20706;
tel. 301 459 3366; fax 301 429 5746; www.nbnbooks.com

Australian agent/distributor: Pan Macmillan Australia, Level 18, St Martins Tower, 31 Market St, Sydney, NSW 2000;
tel. 1300 135 113; fax 1300 135 103; customer.service@macmillan.com.au

New Zealand agent/distributor: David Bateman Ltd, 50 Tarndale Grove, Off Bush Road, Albany, Auckland; tel. (09) 415 7664; fax (09) 415 8892

Publisher: Joanna Lorenz
Managing Editor: Linda Fraser
Editor: Sarah Uttridge
Authors: Michael Bright, John Farndon, Dr Jen Green, Tom Jackson, Robin Kerrod, Rhonda Klevansky, Barbara Taylor
Illustrators: Julian Baker, Peter Bull, Vanessa Card, Stuart Carter, Rob Sheffield, Sarah Smith, David Webb
Designers: Joyce Mason, Alix Wood

Previously published as *Living In The Wild*

1 3 5 7 9 10 8 6 4 2

PICTURE CREDITS

NOTES

NOTES

NOTES

NOTES

NOTES

Notes

NOTES

NOTES